Bible Names for Your Baby

Bible Names
for Your Baby

Joy Gardner and Paul Gardner

A Liturgical Press Book

THE LITURGICAL PRESS
Collegeville, Minnesota

First published in Great Britain in 1996 by Marshall Pickering, an imprint of HarperCollins*Publishers* under the title *Bible Names for Your Baby*.

© 1996 Joy Gardner & Paul Gardner

Published in the United States of America and in Canada by The Liturgical Press, Collegeville, MN 56321.

The text of The Liturgical Press edition of this book has been adapted from the original by Nancy McDarby.

		3	4	5	6	7	8

Library of Congress Cataloging-in-Publication Data

Gardner, Joy, Doctor.
    Bible names for your baby / Joy Gardner and Paul Gardner.
       p. cm.
      ISBN 0-8146-2704-8 (alk. paper)
      1. Names in the Bible Dictionaries. 2. Names, Personal Dictionaries. I. Gardner, Paul, 1950– . II. Title.
BS435.G37   2000
929.4'4—dc21

99-28697
CIP

To all Joy's grandchildren, who are a real "joy" and who are growing up in families where they are taught about knowing and loving Jesus.

Also to Danielle, Paul's personal assistant. For years she has typed for Paul and organized his life. As she finished typing this book, she was expecting her second child. We wait to see what she calls her baby!

About the authors and the book

Appropriately for a book like this, the authors are a mother and son. Joy Gardner has recently retired from medical practice, where she spent much of her career as a doctor watching over children. She was good at this, given the practice she had with four of her own! She and her late husband, David, named their children after characters in the Bible: Paul, Andrew, Ruth, and John. Hers is a Christian family in which all her children and, later, their marriage partners also came to share the same faith. She now has twelve grandchildren whom she greatly enjoys, especially when she can go home when she feels too exploited as a babysitter!

Paul, married to Sharon, is responsible for three of Joy's grandchildren. He is an Anglican minister in Cheshire in England. He too has named his children after Bible characters: Jonathan, David, and Hannah. Paul thinks writing can be a gentle break from his work of preaching and teaching, until the dreaded publishing deadlines arrive. Then he is extremely grateful for the patience of his family. Perhaps this is why he thought the name "Patience" ought to be included in this volume! He is the editor of a much larger and deeper work on all the characters of the Bible called *The Complete Who's Who of the Bible* (published in 1995). It was while talking to his mother over breakfast one morning about the larger volume that they dreamed up this volume. They both hope its readers will find it useful.

One other thing. Do remember, when you have been woken from sleep for the fourth or fifth time in one night, that in the Bible children are regarded as a very special "heritage from the LORD" (Ps 127:3-4)!

A

Aaron

Meaning: possibly from the Hebrew, "mountaineer"

Aaron was the middle child of the family, coming between Miriam, his older sister, and Moses, his renowned younger brother (Exod 6:20). God appointed him to be the first high priest of the Israelites. He was weak on several occasions when he should have been strong. While Moses was on Mount Sinai, Aaron allowed the Israelites to make a golden calf and worship it (Exod 32). He failed to discipline his sons when they were badly behaved, and they grew up to be ungodly men. Aaron died before the Israelites reached the land of Canaan.

Abel

Meaning: from the Hebrew, "breath" or "vanity"

Abel, the second son of Adam and Eve, was a shepherd. He offered some of his sheep as a sacrifice to God. God was pleased with this and accepted it. His brother Cain also offered a sacrifice, but this proved to be unacceptable to God, probably because Cain's heart was not in it. This made Cain jealous of Abel and very angry. He lured Abel out into the fields, where he killed him (Gen 4:1-8).

Abel is mentioned again in the New Testament, where he is held up as an example of a man of faith. If you hope your child may grow up with faith in God, then this could be a very appropriate name for him.

Abigail

Meaning: from the Hebrew, "my father rejoices"

Variation: Abby, Gail

Abigail would be a wonderful name for your daughter! It means "my father rejoices," and the Bible says that Abigail was beautiful and intelligent. What more could anyone want?

She was married to a bad-tempered farmer called Nabal. David (before he became the king of Israel) had protected Nabal's shepherds and flocks from attack in the desert, but when David's men asked Nabal for some food, he sent back an insulting refusal.

Abigail heard that David's men were coming to Nabal's farm to take vengeance. She quietly went out to meet the oncoming troops and gave them some food for a feast, pleading with David not to massacre Nabal's household. David appreciated the way Abigail had held him back from bloodshed. He thanked her for the food and sent her home peacefully. Soon after this Nabal died. When David heard of his death, he sent for Abigail, and they were married (1 Sam 25).

She was a fine woman—sensible, intelligent, loyal, and discreet. Certainly, any father with a daughter like this would rejoice. Whether your daughter will ever become a queen is another matter!

Abraham

Meaning: from the Hebrew, "father of many"

Variation: Abe, Abie

Give a baby this name, and you never know what might happen! Abraham is one of the most famous names in both Christianity and Judaism. He was an extraordinary traveller who journeyed with his entire extended family and all his flocks all the way from Haran in Mesopotamia (modern-day Iraq) to Canaan (modern-day Israel), where he eventually settled down. This journey took years to complete, and he made it not because he had itchy feet but rather because God told him to go.

Abraham must have had a strong faith in God because he didn't actually know where God was taking him when he set off. Also, he happened to be seventy-five years old at the time—this journey was a big undertaking for a senior citizen! It's interesting to speculate what the other members of his family thought about Abraham's decision to leave Haran. Did they have some faith in God too, or did they just think Abraham was crazy?

But God had very special plans for this man of faith. He was to become the founder of a whole nation of people who would later be called "Israel." Later still, these Israelites were to be called "Jews." The New Testament says that Christians too are descendants of Abraham. This is not because every Christian has to be Jewish by birth but because Abraham is the ancestor of all people who have true faith in God. Most importantly, of course, it was one of Abraham's descendants who was going to be the Savior of the world, for Jesus Christ was born into a Jewish family.

Abraham was married to a beautiful woman called Sarah. They went through many hardships together and Abraham's behavior was by no means always perfect, but his faith in God helped them both through the hard times.

Any boy growing up with the name Abraham would have a lot to live up to, but if you want to encourage your son to have a deep faith in God and to have an adventurous spirit, then this might be just the name for him. Certainly, you would have some wonderful bedside stories to tell him about his famous namesake's amazing travels and complete trust in God.

You can read about Abraham's fascinating life in Genesis 12–25.

Absalom

Meaning: from the Hebrew, "father of peace"

If Absalom were alive today, we might think he was like a hippie from the sixties! He was renowned for his beauty and his long hair, and his life was wild and passionate (2 Sam 14:25-27). He was a royal prince, the third of King David's sons. Apparently indiscretion among younger royals is nothing new!

David's eldest son, Amnon, raped Absalom's sister, Tamar. After two years of seething anger and resentment, during which no punishment had been exacted, Absalom killed Amnon in a revenge attack. After this murder Absalom had to go into exile. Eventually, when he returned, he conspired to overthrow his father King David. In a battle between Absalom's troops and those loyal to David, Absalom fled on his horse. As he passed under some low trees, his long hair, which must have been flowing out behind him as he rode, got caught in some branches, and he was left hanging by his hair with no horse to support him. In spite of David's instructions to the contrary, his army commander, Joab, found Absalom and seized the opportunity to kill him. David was distraught. He had always hoped that he and his son could be reconciled (see 2 Sam 18).

While Absalom is not a particularly good example for any child, he was a son who, for all his waywardness, was adored by his father. Almost any son, during his teenage years, is going to have a touch of Absalom in him!

Adam

Meaning: **from the Hebrew, "human being" in general, or specifically the name of the first man**

What was it like to be the very first man on earth? The Bible tells us that Adam was the first man whom God created (Gen 1:26-27). He was placed by God in the beautiful Garden of Eden, where God talked directly to him. God created the woman Eve to be Adam's helper and support. Together they were meant to enjoy the marvellous world which God had created. They were to rule it and to care for it and for the animals. Sadly, they ruined this paradise by disobeying God, and they were ejected from the Garden of Eden. Because Adam was the "father" of all humanity, so all humanity inherited that disobedience and stood in need of God's forgiveness.

The New Testament calls Jesus Christ the "last Adam" (see 1 Cor 15:45)—in other words, a second Adam. This is because with Jesus, God was giving humanity a whole new start. Where Adam had sinned when tested, Jesus did not sin. Where Adam had not led humanity in the right direction, Jesus did. Jesus died on the cross to save people from the sin which Adam had introduced into the world.

Adam is a popular name these days, but few people understand how significant it is. To name a child Adam and to teach him that there was a "last Adam" who died for the sin of men and women would be a lovely permanent reminder to the child of Jesus' love and forgiveness.

Adriel

Meaning: **from the Hebrew, "God is my majesty"**

This name sounds pleasant, but it would be a very unusual name to give your young son. Only one person was given this name in the Bible, and he was the man who married King Saul's daughter, Merab, whom Saul had originally promised to David (1 Sam 18:19; 2 Sam 21:8). He does not seem to have had a very happy life—certainly not one you would wish on your child!

Agabus

Meaning: **possibly from the Hebrew, "to love"**

This name may not be well known, but it has a good biblical pedigree! In the New Testament, Agabus was one of the early Christians. He was given two specific "prophecies" or messages from God. First, he foretold a famine which would spread through the Roman world. The Christians in Antioch immediately began a collection to help to feed the Christians living in Judea and Jerusalem.

Many churches contributed, and the gift was taken to Jerusalem by Barnabas and Paul. Secondly, Agabus came to Paul in Caesarea and told him that if he went to Jerusalem, he would be imprisoned. This prophecy, of course, came true, and Paul was later arrested and eventually went to Rome for trial (see Acts 11 and 21).

This would be an interesting and unusual name for a child, and could remind a family of the need to be faithful to God in all circumstances and that God may use anyone in God's service.

Alexander

Meaning: from the Greek "defender and protector of men"

Male variations: Alec, Alex, Sander, Sandy

Female variations: Alexandra, Alex, Alexandrina, Alexandrine, Alexia, Sandi, Sandy

This is a "world-beater" of a name! Of course, the most famous Alexander was Alexander the Great, the Greek general who conquered so much of the world for the Greeks. But also several men with this name are mentioned in the New Testament. One was the son of Simon of Cyrene, who carried Jesus' cross (Mark 15:21). Another belonged to the family of the High Priest (Acts 4:6). In Ephesus, an Alexander was involved in the uproar against Paul, who had preached the gospel of Christ in the city (Acts 19:33). In one of his letters to Timothy, the apostle Paul wrote about a man called Alexander who had, unfortunately, fallen away from his Christian faith (1 Tim 1:20). Later, also writing to Timothy, Paul spoke of an Alexander who did him a great deal of harm (2 Tim 4:14).

It's a fine-sounding name, and it was given to kings from time to time, possibly because of Alexander the Great.

Alexandria

Meaning: A place on the northwest coast of Egypt, founded by Alexander the Great in 332 B.C.

Female variations: See Alexander

Male variations: See Alexander

Alexandria is mentioned in Acts 6:9 and 18:24. In the first passage we read of some of the Jews from Alexandria being among those who stirred up opposition to Stephen, the Christian preacher, who became the first martyr. However, in Acts 18:24 we read that this is the city from which the famous Jewish Christian preacher, Apollos, came. He was said to have a "thorough knowledge of the Scriptures."

Amos

Meaning: from the Hebrew, "(burden)-bearer"

This is a fine name for any boy: the biblical Amos is an outstanding role model. He lived in the country in a village called Tekoa, not far from Bethlehem, during the eighth century B.C.E. It seems that he was quite a prosperous businessman-farmer who dealt in sheep and who was also an expert in growing figs. From this background God called him to bear the burden of a message to God's people in the northern kingdom, Israel, because of the sins of injustice and oppression the rich were committing against the poor. He spoke out in criticism of the shrine at Bethel. Amos was very aware that he was just an ordinary man to whom God had given a prophetic message for his day. He condemned the wickedness of the kings and people of his day, calling them to return in faith to the one true God who loved them and cared for them.

Certainly such a selfless and God-honoring man provides us with a very worthy name for any boy. Who knows? Maybe your child will grow up to be a fearless man of faith who will speak out God's truth to his generation! (See the book of Amos.)

Anah

Meaning: possibly from the Hebrew, "nephew"

This is probably not a name you will want to use. It sounds similar to the familiar girls' names Hannah and Anna, but in fact Anah is a man's name in the Old Testament. Two men of this name are mentioned (Gen 36:2, 29), and neither has an Israelite background. The first was the father of the Canaanite woman whom Esau married, much against his father's wishes! This name would be unsuitable for a boy these days, as he would be teased for having a girl's name, even though it is spelt differently!

Anan

Meaning: from the Hebrew, "cloud"

Anan was one of the leaders of the Jews who in Nehemiah's day sealed an agreement to worship and obey only God the Lord (Neh 10:26). This would be an unusual name for a boy today, but it might encourage him to grow up to worship and obey God.

Andrew

Meaning: from the Greek, "manly"

Male variation: Andy

Female variation: Andrea

Most boys like to be thought of as "manly," so this name should please your son as he grows up. In the New Testament a man named Andrew was a disciple of John the Baptist, but he then became the very first disciple to be called by Jesus (John 1:40-44). He must have been a man full of faith, for he immediately followed Jesus and then quickly brought his brother Peter to meet Jesus too.

Like Peter, and the brothers James and John, Andrew was a fisherman. He was probably a likeable and approachable person, for he and Phillip spoke to Jesus when some Greek-speaking Jews asked to see Jesus (John 12:22). It was Andrew who knew about the boy with his loaves and fishes when food was needed to feed the crowds who had come to hear Jesus teach (John 6:1-15).

Anna

Meaning: Greek, from Hebrew, "Hannah," "favored" or "grace"

Variations: Annie, Anica, Anne, Annette, Anita. See also Hannah

A woman named Anna is mentioned by St. Luke in his account of the birth and childhood of Jesus. She was a prophet, and after seven years of marriage she became a widow and spent all her time in the Temple, serving the Lord. When she was eighty-four years old, Mary and Joseph brought the baby Jesus to the Temple, and under the guidance of the Holy Spirit, Anna recognized that the tiny baby was the long-awaited Messiah. She praised God and told everyone she met all about the baby she had seen (Luke 2:36-38).

Anna must have been a woman who loved God deeply. All the years of her life, which must have held many sorrows and hardships, she had worshipped and prayed and waited for God to send the Messiah. She would be a wonderful person to be named after.

Asaph

Meaning: from the Hebrew, "to gather"

This would be an unusual name, but it might be very suitable for a son who was likely to be musical. Asaph was a Levite (the Levites were an Israelite tribe of priests and temple servers) whom King David put in charge of the singing in the Temple in Jerusalem (1 Chron 6:31-40). His name is mentioned in the titles of some of the psalms in the Bible. Perhaps he wrote them, or they may have been written for him.

Asher

Meaning: from the Hebrew, "fortunate, happy"

This name has a charming meaning, though it is certainly uncommon these days. Asher was very important in the history of Israel. He was the eighth of Jacob's twelve sons, so he became the head of one of the twelve tribes of Israel (Gen 30:13).

Augustus

Meaning: from the Latin, "majestic," "worthy of honor"

Male variations: Augustine, Austen, Austin, Gus

Female variations: Augusta, Augustina, Austine, Gussie

By stretching things a little, we can perhaps call this a "Bible name." Luke 2:1 tells us that Augustus was the Roman emperor who ordered a census to be taken at the time of Jesus' birth. In Christianity the name is perhaps most famous not because of the Emperor Augustus but because of the famous Christian preacher Augustine of Hippo, who lived in the fourth century C.E.

B

Barnabas

Meaning: from the Aramaic, "son of encouragement" or "son of consolation"

Variations: Barnabie, Barnie, Barney

What a wonderful name for your child! In the Bible this was a sort of surname or nickname given by the apostles to a man named Joseph, a Jew from Cyprus who had become a Christian. His new name was meant to be a reflection on his character, so he must have been a fine friend. When Saul was converted and the other Christians were reluctant to believe it, it was Barnabas who encouraged them to accept him. We all love to know people who always find something encouraging to say! Barnabas was kind and generous and was good at understanding people and sympathizing with their needs and troubles.

He worked in Antioch with the apostle Paul and then travelled with him for a while on his missionary journeys. Later he worked closely with John Mark (the writer of Mark's Gospel) as he travelled, preaching the gospel of Jesus. The Bible says he was a good man, "full of the Holy Spirit and of faith." He would be a wonderful example for a namesake to follow. (See especially Acts 14–15).

Bartholomew

Meaning: from the Aramaic, "son of Tolmai"

Variations: Bart, Barth, Tolly, Tolomey

This pleasant name is not uncommon these days. Bartholomew was one of the twelve apostles (Matt 10:3). He would have travelled with Jesus, listened to his teaching, and seen his miracles, though we have no records of any particular incidents in which Bartholomew was specially involved.

Bartimaeus

Meaning: from the Aramaic, "son of Timaeus"

Variation: Bart

This man's faith in Jesus would make his name worth remembering as a possible name for your son. He was a blind man who sat begging by the road to Jericho. As Jesus was leaving the city, Bartimaeus shouted loudly to attract his attention, calling him the "Son of David" (Mark 10:46-52), which suggests that he believed that Jesus was the promised Messiah. When Jesus asked what he wanted, Bartimaeus asked for his sight. He seemed to have no doubt at all that Jesus could grant it. Jesus commended him for his faith, and Bartimaeus, now completely healed and able to see, set off along the road with Jesus.

Baruch

Meaning: from the Hebrew, "blessed"

In Old Testament times it was men who were the secretaries. Times are changing, so perhaps your son will be a secretary one day! Of course, the duties of a secretary were not well defined, and Baruch seems to have been not only a secretary but also a general helper and legal adviser to the famous prophet Jeremiah (Jer 32:12-13, 16).

Although convinced that God would judge the people in Judah by sending them into exile, Jeremiah knew that God would later bring them back to Jerusalem, so he showed his trust in God's promises by buying a field. He gave the deeds to Baruch to keep in a sealed jar until his words came true. Jeremiah also dictated to Baruch all that the Lord had told him over the years, and he told Baruch to read it out in the Temple so that the people would be warned. When the king heard about the reading, he took the scroll and burnt it. Jeremiah and Baruch, with great determination, and in real fear for their lives, promptly wrote out the scroll again! (See Jer 36).

Baruch is an unusual name, but the man who held it was greatly used by God. His work helped to preserve Jeremiah's prophecies in a time of great opposition. If you name your son Baruch, you will want to tell him the great biblical stories about his brave namesake and Jeremiah as they stood up for God in the face of persecution. But be careful not to make them bedtime stories, or your young Baruch might have nightmares!

Benjamin

Meaning: **from the Hebrew, "son of my right hand"**

Variations: Ben, Benny, Benjie, Benjy

Benjamin was the second son of Rachel, the wife whom the patriarch Jacob loved dearly. She died as the baby was born and called him Ben-oni, which means "son of sorrow," but Jacob later changed his name. He and his brother Joseph, left without their mother, were very precious to their father and were very close to each other (Gen 35:18, 24).

In later years there was a great famine in Canaan, where they lived. So Benjamin's brothers went down to Egypt to buy grain, though Jacob did not allow Benjamin to accompany them. Unknown to them, when they began to buy grain they were in fact dealing with their brother Joseph, whom they had sold into slavery but who was now the governor of Egypt. Joseph insisted that Benjamin come with them on their next visit. On that second occasion, with great emotion, Joseph made himself known to his brothers, and especially to Benjamin (Gen 45).

Throughout this whole story in the Bible, it becomes clear just how much Benjamin's father loved him and cared for him. If you were to name your child by this name, it would certainly point to how important your baby boy will be in your life—a boy much loved by his parents. However, if you do have other children, be careful that you don't make this child your favorite in the way Jacob did with his Benjamin, the last of his twelve sons!

Bernice

Meaning: from the Greek, "bringer of victory." A Greek name widely known in the Greek and Roman world

Variation: Berenice

Bernice is a very pretty girl's name. Bernice in the Bible was the sister of Herod Agrippa II. The two of them came to Caesarea to visit Governor Festus and were interested in the legal case concerning Festus' prisoner, the apostle Paul. Paul was called before them to explain his Christian faith. Both Bernice and Agrippa were of Jewish birth, although they were Roman aristocrats. They listened carefully to Paul, and later agreed together that he had done nothing that deserved death or imprisonment (see Acts 25:23; 26:30).

Beryl

Meaning: a word found in various languages. In Greek it meant "a green jewel" while in Sanskrit it meant "precious stones." In Arabic the word referred to a "crystal."

This word has become a well-known girl's name. Any girl with this name would love to hear that in the Bible the precious stone beryl is associated with beauty and preciousness to God. The garments made at God's direction for Aaron the high priest included a breastpiece adorned with twelve precious stones. On each was engraved the name of one of the tribes of Israel, the significance being that they were borne on Aaron's heart before the Lord. One of these stones was a beryl (Exod 28:20). In the book of Revelation the apostle John had a vision of the holy city, the New Jerusalem. The foundations of the city's walls were decorated with many precious stones, including beryl (Rev 21:20).

Bethany

Meaning: from the Hebrew, "the house of figs"

Recently this has become quite a popular girl's name, but in the Bible, Bethany was actually the name of a village about two miles from Jerusalem on the road from Jericho. It was here that Lazarus and his sisters Mary and Martha lived. Jesus loved this family and stayed in their home. It was here that he remonstrated with Martha about being too busy while Mary made time to listen to his teaching (Luke 10:38-42).When Lazarus died, the sisters sent for Jesus, who came to Bethany and raised him from the dead after he had been in the grave for four days (John 11).

Bethany is an attractive name for a girl, reminding us of a place of real significance in the life of Christ.

Boaz

Meaning: **from the Hebrew, "strength" or "swiftness"**

Boaz was a godly landowner in the days of the Judges (see the book of Ruth). He was related to Naomi's husband Elimelech. In a time of severe famine, Naomi and Elimelech went to the land of Moab. Here their two sons married, but in time Elimelech and both the sons died. When Naomi and one of her daughters-in-law, Ruth, returned to Bethlehem, Boaz, a generous-hearted and godly man with a strong sense of family, went out of his way to be kind to them and eventually married Ruth. Boaz and Ruth were ancestors of King David.

This would be a very unusual name for your boy, but he would almost certainly be the only Boaz in his class at school! Boaz was a fine character whose life-story could be told again and again to a young child.

Bunni

Meaning: **not known**

This name has nothing to do with rabbits! The Old Testament mentions three Levites (members of the Israelite priestly tribe) called Bunni, all of whom resettled in Jerusalem after the exile in Babylon. They appear to have been committed to God and faithful in their desire to serve. One of them was one of the men who signed the agreement to worship only the Lord God (Neh 9:4; 10:15; 11:15).

C

Caleb

Meaning: from the Hebrew, "bold" or "impetuous"

You may not wish your baby son to be "impetuous," but you might want him to have the character of the biblical Caleb.

In the Old Testament Caleb is first mentioned as one of the men who were sent to spy out the land of Canaan, which the Israelites were at last approaching. Ten of the twelve spies were overwhelmed by the difficulties which would have to be overcome in capturing the land. They were especially afraid of the tall, giant-like people who lived there, and advised against attack (Num 13:26–14:4). Caleb and Joshua alone were certain that God would empower the Israelites for the battle so that they could capture the land which God had promised to them so many years before. As judgment on their lack of faith, the Israelites wandered for forty years in the desert, till all those who had refused to enter the land were dead. Only Joshua and Caleb lived long enough to enter the land. Caleb himself led the fighting against the giant-sized Anakites in the area of Hebron. He was then eighty-five years old, but the Bible says "he wholeheartedly followed the Lord" (Josh 14:14).

He was a sturdy and upright character who was still faithful to God and bold and impetuous even at the age of eighty-five!

Candace

Meaning: the official title of an Ethiopian queen

Variations: Candy, Candie, Kandace

This attractive name is found in Acts 8:27. It was not a personal name, but was the title by which the queen or, more likely, the queen mother of Ethiopia was known. This would be a regal name to give your daughter!

Candace is mentioned in Acts in the story of one of her senior servants, a treasury official. This man was probably a God-fearer, a non-Jew who believed in God, and was returning home after a visit to Jerusalem to worship. He was clearly serious about the Jewish faith and had perhaps met up with some Christians while in Jerusalem. While travelling in his carriage and reading part of the book of Isaiah, he was joined by Philip, a Christian evangelist who had been preaching further north in Samaria. Philip explained that the passage which the man was reading was talking about Jesus Christ. The Ethiopian believed what Philip told him and committed his life to Christ, asking if he could immediately be baptized. This was probably how the gospel first came to Ethiopia, where it quickly took root and spread.

Carmel

Meaning: from the Hebrew, "fruitful land"

Female variations: Carmela, Carma, Carmelina

Male variations: Carmelo, Karmel

Carmel is the name of a range of limestone hills in Israel that extends for around thirty miles southeast from the Bay of Acre on the Mediterranean coast. This was the area where the lovely Abigail lived before she became David's wife. Carmel is most famous, though, for being the place where Elijah challenged the prophets of Baal (1 Kgs 18:20-46). Down through the ages this place-name has also been used as a name for both girls and boys.

Charity

Meaning: from the Latin, "love"

The meaning of this word has changed so much that few parents now choose it as a name for their daughter—which is a pity, given the power and beauty of the original meaning of the word. Today "charity" makes us think of a rather condescending order of giving. However, in New Testament times Christians used the Greek word *agape* to refer to the special kind of love which they had for one another. It was love based on God's love for them—infinite, tender, generous, forgiving, and unconditional. We all need to love like that! Modern translations of the Bible now simply use "love" to translate *agape*, but in older translations the word "charity" was commonly used (see 1 Cor 13). If you would like your daughter to be a warm-hearted, outgoing, generous person, you could not choose a better name.

Cherith

The Cherith was a small river on the eastern side of the River Jordan in the days of the prophet Elijah. When he was fleeing from King Ahab during a time of drought in Israel, Elijah was led by God to this river, and there God kept him alive. The river kept flowing and God sent ravens to bring him bread and meat to eat. The drought was part of God's judgment on the Israelite nation and especially on the sin of King Ahab (see 1 Kgs 17:1-6).

So the name Cherith suggests to us God's generous provision. There are times in life when we all need to discover a Cherith where we can find peace from the craziness of the world and nourishment for our inner being.

Perhaps a daughter with this name might grow up to be someone who will offer comfort and strength to those who are in trouble.

Chloe

Meaning: from the Greek, "green grass"

Variations: Clea, Cloe

The fledgling church at Corinth, one of the most cosmopolitan Mediterranean seaports, caused the apostle Paul more than the usual headache. It was a message sent from Chloe's household that first alerted Paul to some of the problems and quarrels that were going on there. We know nothing about Chloe, yet the mention of her household and her servants suggests that she was a successful businesswoman, of whom there were many in the Roman Empire in those days. It is likely that she was an intelligent, sensible, and practical Christian woman who worshiped in the Corinthian church (1 Cor 1:11) and who, when something was plainly wrong, was unafraid to tackle the problem and call for help.

Christian

Meaning: **This name comes from the title "Christ," which is a Greek translation of the Hebrew word "Messiah," which means "anointed one."**

Male variations: Chris, Christen, Christie, Kristian

Female variations: Christine, Cristine, Kristine, Christina, Tina, Christiana, Chrissie, Kirsty. (The name Christine is not actually to be found in the Bible, which surprises many people!)

It was at Antioch in Syria that the people who believed in Jesus as the Christ or Savior were first called "Christians" (Acts 11:26). No doubt when it was first coined by their opponents, the name was meant to be a derisive nickname. However, it soon caught on since Christians were proud to be known as followers of their Lord Jesus. The name was used by King Agrippa, who said that the apostle Paul had almost persuaded him to become a Christian (Acts 26:28). In one of his letters the apostle Peter wrote that Christians should endure suffering for the sake of their faith and yet also thank God that they bear the name "Christian" (1 Pet 4:16).

This name and its variants have been given to boys and girls for a very long time. If you give this name to your child, he or she will have a high calling indeed.

Claudia

Meaning: **Female variation of Claudius, meaning "lame"**

Variations: Claudette, Claudine

Claudia was a friend of the apostle Paul and of Timothy. While Paul was in prison in Rome, he wrote a letter to Timothy, and Claudia joined Paul in sending greetings (2 Tim 4:21). This was probably written right at the end of the apostle's life, just before he was put to death for his Christian faith. Perhaps Claudia was one of the few friends who were there in those last days to comfort and help Paul at a lonely and sad time in his life. No doubt she was a fearless woman who was prepared to be known as a Christian at a time of severe persecution.

Claudius

Meaning: **from the Latin, "lame"**

Variations: Claud, Claude

Two men by this name are mentioned in the New Testament, but neither offers a good role model for a growing child! The fourth Roman emperor (A.D. 41–54) was named Claudius. He succeeded Caligula, who had deeply offended the Jews by making a statue of himself and intending to have it erected in the Temple in Jerusalem (he died before this could happen). Claudius was not quite as bad to the Jews as Caligula, but he did eject the Jews from the city of Rome (Acts 18:2). A man named Claudius Lysias, a Roman official, is mentioned in Acts 23:26-30. He was a tribune responsible for the garrison in Jerusalem, where the apostle Paul was held captive after his arrest. He seems to have been reasonably fair to Paul and protected him from some very antagonistic crowds.

Clement

Meaning: from the Latin, "mild" or "merciful"

Male variation: Clem

Female variations: Clemence, Clemency

Clement was a member of the church at Philippi and is spoken of as one of the apostle Paul's "co-workers," so perhaps he had helped to found the church there (Phil 4:3). Paul writes that he is sure that Clement's name is "in the book of life." A few decades later a famous bishop of Rome was called by this name, but it is unlikely that he was the same person.

If you choose this name for your son or daughter, it would be good to pray for them too that their name will be "in the book of life"—that is, that they will belong to God forever.

Cornelius

Meaning: from the Latin *corneus*, which can be a certain tree. The word can also mean "hard-hearted" and "insensitive"

Male variations: Cornie, Cornell

Female variation: Cornelia

Given the latter meaning, this might not be a name you would choose for your child! However, in the New Testament Cornelius was a centurion of influence and repute in the Italian cohort of the Roman army. He was stationed in Caesarea and he and his family worshiped the God of the Jews and were devout and generous to all those who were in need. He had a vision from God in which he was told to send a messenger to Joppa to ask Simon Peter to come over to visit him. At first Peter was reluctant, believing that Gentiles were "unclean" and that he should not associate with them. But God reassured him and he went with the messengers.

When Peter arrived he talked to a large gathering of people in Cornelius' house, telling them about Jesus Christ. Many believed in Christ, and the Holy Spirit came to them, just as it had to the first Jewish believers on the day of Pentecost. Cornelius was thus the first Gentile convert. (See Acts 10.) When Peter went up to Jerusalem to give a report on this to the apostles, they realized that the gospel message was indeed for everyone, both Jew and Gentile.

Crispus

Meaning: from the Latin, "curly-headed"

Male variations: Crispin, Crispian

Female variation: Crispina

Has your baby been born, and are you still trying to choose a name? Well, if he or she has curly hair, then this might be an unusual name that will catch your eye. In the New Testament a Crispus is mentioned living in Corinth. He was a leader in the local Jewish synagogue, where the apostle Paul had begun to preach before being ejected. Crispus, however, was among those Jews who continued to listen to what Paul was saying, and eventually he "became a believer in the Lord, together with all his household" (Acts 18:8). It must have taken great courage to turn to Christ in the midst of such furious persecution. He was prepared to live with whatever was thrown at him for the sake of what he believed to be true. A fine example for any youngster to follow.

Crystal

Variations: Crissie, Crys

This is not a person's name in the Bible, but these days it is used as a girl's name. In the Bible the word "crystal" is particularly used in the book of Revelation. The apostle John, the writer of the book, had visions of heaven, and he saw the throne of God surrounded by a sea of glass "like crystal" (Rev 4:6). From the throne of God flowed the water of life, which was "bright as crystal." So the name Crystal reminds us of some wonderful biblical imagery and would make a beautiful name for a baby girl.

D

Damaris

Meaning: **from a Greek word that implies "gentleness"**

Variation: Damara

This is a very pretty name for a girl, and it used to be popular. Damaris lived in Athens and was one of the few people who were converted to Christianity through Paul's preaching when he was there. As she is specially mentioned in the book of Acts, it may be that she was a prominent and well-known woman in the city (Acts 17:34).

Dan

Meaning: **from the Hebrew, "judge" or "judgment"**

Female variation: Dana

Dan was one of the sons of Jacob. He was actually the son of Rachel's servant Bilhah, but he would have been considered as Rachel's own child. Rachel was so pleased with his birth that she named him Dan, meaning that God had vindicated her or judged in her favor. At last God had given her a son, just as he had given one to Leah, Jacob's other wife (Gen 30:5-6).

Although Dan is often just a shortened form of Daniel, there is still every reason to use Dan as a name in its own right.

Daniel

Meaning: from the Hebrew, "God judges"

Male variations: Dan, Danny, Dannie

Female variations: Dannielle, Daniella, Dana, Danella, Danita

Daniel is best known for the incident where God saved him from death when he was thrown into a den of lions, but throughout his life Daniel faithfully served the Lord and obeyed God's commands without regard for the consequences. When he was still a young man he was taken as a captive from Jerusalem to Babylon. He was selected to be trained for service in the Babylonian government, and he rose to be a powerful man in a career that lasted over sixty years.

God gave him the ability to interpret dreams, and he also had visions of things that were to come. Everyone knew that he prayed three times every day to his God. Jealous of him and seeking his downfall, other government officials persuaded the king to make it an offence to pray to anyone other than the king himself for thirty days. When they saw Daniel at his window praying to God as usual, they insisted that he be thrown into the lion's den. But God kept Daniel safe, and the lions did not harm him. (See the book of Daniel.)

What an excellent name for a boy or girl! It would symbolize your hopes and prayers that he or she will grow up to be a faithful and fearless witness to God, just as the biblical Daniel was.

David

Meaning: this is not altogether clear, but the name probably comes from the Hebrew, "beloved"

Male variations: Dave, Davey

Female variations: Davene, Davida, Davita

David was a biblical character with great appeal. We first meet him as the youngest son in a family of seven sons. He had the lowliest job—watching sheep in the fields. He played music, sang, and wrote wonderful songs called psalms, which were later sung at the temple worship in Jerusalem and which many people still love to sing today. He was brave and fearless, tackling even the giant Goliath, who had defied the Israelite armies. David spent many years wandering around the country keeping out of the way of King Saul, who wanted to kill him. He is well known for his great friendship with Jonathan, Saul's son. In due course David became king, and he led his armies to many victories as he strengthened and extended the kingdom of Israel.

There were troubles in David's life too. He committed adultery with the wife of one of his army officers, and then he engineered her husband's death in battle. He had trouble with his sons: Absalom rose up against him and actually drove him into exile for a while. (For David's life and times see 1 Sam 16–2 Kgs 1.)

However, in spite of all this, David still loved God with all his heart. When he sinned, he was deeply sorry and asked to be forgiven by God. Many psalms show us how deeply he loved God and how close he was to God. According to God's promise to David, the Lord Jesus Christ was born into the line of his descendants.

No wonder that David has always been among the favorite names for boys! If you give your child this name, then you could pray that God will say about your son what God said about David, "a man after [my] own heart," because he did what God wanted him to do.

Deborah

Meaning: from the Hebrew, "a honey bee"

Variations: Deb, Debbie, Debra

Deborah was one of the judges or rulers of Israel before the time of the kings. She was a godly woman who completely trusted in the Lord and thanked and praised God for all her successes.

The only woman known to have become a judge, she urged Barak to lead an army against Sisera, the general of the Canaanite king, under whose rule the Israelites were living. Barak would only do so if Deborah went with him. They won a great victory, for which Deborah gave glory to God in a great poem known as "the Song of Deborah" (Judg 4–5). She was a very brave person who was prepared to fight for God and God's people, even when others, through lack of faith, were fearful. This woman would give any growing girl a challenge to live up to!

Delilah

Meaning: from the Hebrew, "languishing"

Variations: Delila, Lila, Lilah

This name carries a health warning! Delilah was a beautiful Philistine woman who seduced the Israelite judge, Samson, and wheedled out of him the secret of his great physical strength (see Judg 16).

Delilah is a glamorous biblical character, but she is hardly a good role model, so hers is probably a name you would not choose for your daughter. Besides, in later life she might well object to having been named after a pagan seductress!

Diana

Meaning: from the Latin, "goddess"

Variations: Deanna, Deanne, Di, Diane, Dianna

Diana was the Latin name for the Greek goddess Artemis. The Artemis who was worshiped at Ephesus was an Eastern mother-goddess given the name of the Greek virgin huntress. Those who made a living out of her worshipers by selling them statues and trinkets were intensely opposed to Paul's preaching of the gospel of the true God because they could see that if people became Christians they would no longer be interested in "Diana memorabilia"! In the theater at Ephesus two faithful Christians named Aristarchus and Gaius underwent a dreadful ordeal as a crowd of thousands shouted at them and vented their fury on them (Acts 19). Diana is a popular name today, but some parents would not wish to give it to their daughter because it is the name of a pagan goddess.

Dinah

Meaning: from the Hebrew, "judge"

Variations: Sometimes this name is confused with Diana and is similarly shortened to names such as Di, Dina, Deanna

Dinah was the daughter of Leah and Jacob. The son of the ruler of Shechem captured Dinah and raped her. After this horrific attack, he wanted to marry her and offered to do anything for her family if only they would allow the marriage. The Israelites were, however, forbidden by God to intermarry with non-Israelites. Simeon and Levi, two of Dinah's brothers, were very angry about their sister's plight and planned their revenge. They agreed to the marriage on the condition that all the men of Shechem were circumcised. Perhaps surprisingly, the men of Shechem went along with this proposal. However, while they were still in pain after the circumcision, the two brothers attacked the city and killed all the male inhabitants (Gen 34).

This story is full of sadness and horror, and it might well put anyone off choosing this name for their baby girl. However, Dinah was part of the great family of Jacob, and she was certainly loved by her brothers.

Dorcas

Meaning: from the Greek, "gazelle." See also "Tabitha"

Dorcas lived in Joppa in the days of the apostles, and she showed her love for God by helping the poor and especially by making clothes for them. When she died her friends sent for Peter. As they all wept and mourned and talked about Dorcas' goodness, Peter prayed over her, and she returned to life again (Acts 9:36-39).

This would be an unusual name for your baby girl, but it sounds pleasant and it belonged to a very good and godly woman.

Drusilla

Meaning: from the Greek, "soft-eyed"

Variations: Dru, Drussie

This pretty name of Greek origin is out of fashion now. Drusilla was a Jewish woman married to Felix, the governor in Jerusalem. Paul was brought before Felix in the first stage of his trial in Caesarea. After a preliminary hearing, Felix postponed the proceeding. When, some days later, Drusilla came to Caesarea with him, he sent for the apostle and both of them listened as he talked to them about faith in Jesus Christ. Bernice, the sister of King Agrippa, who later heard Paul defending his faith, was also the sister of Drusilla (Acts 24:24).

E

Ebenezer

Meaning: from the Hebrew, "stone of help"

This name might sound rather Dickensian these days, but it has a lovely meaning. In the Old Testament it was a place-name. The prophet Samuel placed a stone, like a boundary marker, between the towns of Mizpah and Shen. This served as a reminder of the fact that it was there that God had led the Israelites to victory over the Philistines. In 1 Samuel 7:12 we read: "Samuel took a stone and . . . named it Ebenezer; for he said, 'Thus far the LORD has helped us.'" Perhaps that is how you feel with your new-born child—"thus far has the Lord helped us!"

Eli

Meaning: from the Hebrew, "God is uplifted"

What better meaning could there be for a name, and yet this is not a common name these days. Sadly, the Eli whom we read about in 1 Samuel 1–4 was not a very praiseworthy character. His story is a cautionary reminder of just how important a father's loving and caring discipline will be in the life of any child. Eli was the priest at the Israelite center of worship at Shiloh at around the time of the prophet Samuel's birth. He combined the role of priest with legal responsibilities as one of the judges of Israel for eighteen years. He was the one who had overheard Hannah's tears as she cried to God for a baby. He was the one who later told Hannah's son Samuel that the voice he had heard in the middle of the night must have been God speaking. His heart seemed to be in the right place and he cared passionately for his country. But in the midst of all his work, he neglected his sons, and when he tried to discipline them, they took no notice. When they were older, they committed immoral acts even within the precincts of the sanctuary, and God judged the nation as a result.

Elijah

Meaning: from the Hebrew, "my God is the Lord"

Variations: Elias, Elie

This is not a very common name these days, but a boy could feel proud to be named after this famous Old Testament prophet. Parents would have a host of exciting bedtime stories to tell their son about the life of this prophet.

In keeping with his name, Elijah was totally committed to his God (see especially 1 Kgs 17–19). God gave him the dangerous task of bringing messages of judgment to the wicked King Ahab. With God's help, Elijah did what God asked of him, thus bringing upon himself the wrath of Ahab and his wife Jezebel. God enabled Elijah to perform miracles, and his life was preserved by God in miraculous ways. When he was fleeing from Ahab during the great drought that was God's judgment on the evil king, God ensured that the prophet was kept safe and well fed. Birds brought him food and God showed him a small brook that did not dry up.

His extraordinary faith and commitment to God was most clearly seen on Mount Carmel. There, at God's command, he challenged the prophets of the pagan god known as Baal. Both parties set up altars with a sacrifice on top. The challenge was to call down fire from heaven to burn up the sacrifice. This would reveal who was the most powerful—God or Baal. Though the pagan prophets tried all morning to make their god bring fire, nothing happened. Elijah then had them pour water over his altar and sacrifice until it was completely saturated. He then prayed just once to God, and fire came down, burning up his sacrifice and even the altar of the pagan prophets!

In spite of seeing God's great power in many different ways, Elijah was also intensely human and frequently had very serious times of doubt and worry. Often he was very lonely, and sometimes he was depressed. He had to learn that God was always with him. On Mount Horeb, God drew near to him to reassure and comfort him. God spoke to him not in some dramatic way—through fire, wind, or earthquake—but in "sheer silence" (see 1 Kgs 19).

Elizabeth

Meaning: from the Hebrew, "my God is my oath"

Variations: Bab, Bessie, Beth, Betsie, Bett, Bette, Betty, Elisa, Elisabet, Elisabeth, Elise, Elisheva, Eliza, Elizabet, Elsa, Elspet, Isabel, Lisa, Lizbeth

This has always been a favorite name for a girl. How good to be named after such a faithful woman, who was so understanding and compassionate and so prepared to follow God's plan for her life.

Elizabeth was the wife of a priest called Zechariah. Both were well on in years, but they had no children. One day, when he was performing his duties in the Temple, an angel appeared to Zechariah to tell him that Elizabeth would have a baby. Because he was very doubtful about this, the angel told Zechariah that he would be dumb until the boy had been born and had been named "John." In due course this came to pass, and so John the Baptist came into the world. Elizabeth was related to Mary the mother of Jesus, and it was to Elizabeth that Mary went when she knew that she too was going to bear a child.

Elizabeth was a woman who loved God deeply. Her greeting to Mary ("Blessed are you among women, and blessed is the fruit of your womb") showed that she was aware that both of them were involved in the Messiah's coming into the world, and in this they rejoiced. We are told that when the pregnant Mary arrived to visit, Elizabeth's own child leaped in her womb "for joy." The older Elizabeth and the much younger Mary, both expecting their first child, then looked after each other for three months. How they must have talked about what was going to happen, about the coming Messiah and about John, whose special job would be to prepare the way for Jesus (Luke 1–2).

Emerald

Meaning: a brilliant green stone

This is not the name of a person in the Bible but is often used as a girl's name these days. In the Old Testament an emerald was one of the precious stones on the breast-plate worn by the Israelite high priest. These jewels represented the twelve tribes of Israel, held upon the priest's heart before God (Exod 28:17). When the apostle John describes his vision of the New Jerusalem in the book of Revelation, he mentions emeralds in the foundations (Rev 21:19).

Enoch

Meaning: from the Hebrew, "teacher"

Enoch was one of the figures in the earliest chapters of biblical history. We are told that he "walked with God" and that he did not die but God simply took him away (Gen 5:24). What an interesting person! He had faith, although he could not have known much about God, and he led a righteous life. Enoch would perhaps be an unusual name, but it would be a great reminder for a growing child of the importance of following in the ways of God and leading a righteous life.

Eran

Meaning: not known

This is indeed an uncommon name, though attractive. It has been used for both men and women in the past, but it is a man's name on the one occasion when it occurs in the Bible. Eran was a grandson of Ephraim and a descendant, therefore, of Abraham. He became a leader of his own family clan (Num 26:36).

Esther

Meaning: from the Hebrew, "myrtle"

Esther was a young Jewess whose parents had died, leaving her in the care of her cousin Mordecai. They lived in Susa in Persia in the time of King Xerxes. His queen, Vashti, offended her husband, and so the search began for a new queen. Esther was chosen by the King as the most beautiful woman presented to him, though at this time she did not disclose the fact that she was Jewish. Mordecai then discovered that there was a plot to annihilate all the Jews in the Persian empire. He informed Esther, telling her that this was perhaps why God had made her queen, so that she could offer protection to her people. Now, with great courage, she approached the king to seek his help. He graciously listened to her and gave permission for the Jews to defend themselves when the attacks came. They defended themselves well, and the intended massacre did not happen. (For the whole exciting story, see the book of Esther in the Old Testament.)

The Bible tells us that Esther was a very beautiful woman, and a very brave one too. At great personal risk she kept faith with her people and her God. Because of her faithfulness God was able to use her in a dramatic and wonderful way. A lovely name, and a courageous person!

Ethan

Meaning: from the Hebrew, "ancient"

You may not have heard this name before, but it has a good sound about it and would certainly be a distinctive name for your son.

There are actually several men called Ethan in the Bible. One Ethan was renowned for his wisdom, but Solomon was said to be even wiser than him (1 Kgs 4:31). Another Ethan was a Levite who was appointed by David to sing and play the bronze cymbals as the ark of the covenant was brought up to Jerusalem (1 Chr 15:17-19).

Eunice

Meaning: from the Greek, "good victory"

She was a Jewish Christian whose husband was a Greek. She is known to us in the New Testament through her famous son, Timothy. She and her mother or mother-in-law, Lois, brought up young Timothy to know the Scriptures. This wonderful motherly teaching, praised by the apostle Paul, had well prepared Timothy for the work of an evangelist, to which God was later to call him (2 Tim 1:5). Eunice seems to have been a fine Christian woman, and her attractive name would be a good choice for any daughter.

Evangeline

Meaning: from the Greek, "to bring good news"

The birth of a baby is "good news." This girl's name has a happy and joyful meaning and certainly sounds very attractive. The name itself doesn't actually appear in the Bible. However, the New Testament is all about the "evangel" or gospel—the good news about the birth of Jesus and how he brings forgiveness to people and shows the love of God to the world. (See especially Isa 52:7 and Mark 1:15.)

Eve

Meaning: **from the Hebrew, "life." The Bible tells us that this name was given to the first woman by Adam "because she was the mother of all living"**

Variations: Eva, Evie, Evita

This might be just the name to choose if your first child is a girl. The Bible tells us that Eve was the first woman God created. She lived in the Garden of Eden with her husband Adam. In that wonderful paradise they experienced the intimate presence of God, who talked with them and told them about the creation. God created Eve because, without her, the man Adam was incomplete. God's creation needed the complementarity of men and women, not just for procreation but in all sorts of ways that would help them *together* to look after all that God had given them in this world.

However, sadly, Eve and Adam rebelled against God. They listened to Satan, who tempted them to disregard God's commands. This led eventually to God's judgment and their eviction from the Garden of Eden (Gen 1–3).

The tragedy of sin coming into the world is still well known today. But even in the midst of the divine judgment on Satan, Adam, and Eve, God made a wonderfully gracious promise to the woman: one day, one of her descendants would destroy Satan and bring deliverance. God was pointing to the time when another woman, Mary, would give birth to a baby called Jesus. He would bring salvation and forgiveness for sin to all who had faith in him.

Ezra

Meaning: Ezra comes from the Hebrew word, "help," perhaps shortened from "Ezra-yah"—"God helps"

Ezra came from a family of priests and was a Jewish scribe in captivity in Babylon. By permission of the Persian Emperor Artaxerxes he led a big party of exiles back to Jerusalem to rebuild the city and the Temple. When he reached Jerusalem, he was horrified to find that many of the exiles who had already returned were not following God's laws and had intermarried with the surrounding heathen peoples. Ezra called them together, wept and prayed, and read the law to them. They repented, and their leaders signed a promise to keep God's commandments. (See the book of Ezra.)

Ezra was a man whose zeal for God took precedence over anything else. He made the long journey back to Jerusalem and then brought about great reforms in the life of the community. His commitment to God above all else would provide a good example to any child.

Faith

Meaning: **a whole-hearted commitment to and trust in something or someone**

Though "faith" is really only an abstract noun, it has rightly always been popular as a girl's name. The Bible talks about faith in regard to someone completely committing themselves to trust in God or in God's Son Jesus. Faith is a beautiful name with deep meaning.

Felix

Meaning: **from the Latin, "happy"**

Female variations: Felicia, Felice, Felicity

Felix was the name of the Roman procurator of Judea when the apostle Paul was first tried by the Roman authorities (Acts 23:23–24:27). Although he was interested to hear Paul speak about his faith, the book of Acts does not tell us whether he became a Christian.

Felix means "happy" or "joyful," and joy is one of the fruits of the Holy Spirit. So this would make a very positive and encouraging name for a child.

Festus

Meaning: from the Latin, "solemn" or "festive"

The birth of your child will doubtless give you joy and so perhaps may make you think of this name, but the biblical Festus was not really someone to commend highly! He was the Roman procurator of Judea in 60–61 C.E. (Acts 24:27–26:32) and was involved in the trial of the apostle Paul, in which the Jewish leaders had accused Paul of treason. Festus simply thought Paul was insane, but Paul had appealed to the emperor, and so Festus eventually had to see to it that Paul was taken to Rome for his trial.

G

Gabriel

Meaning: from the Hebrew, "God is strong"

Male variation: Gabe

Female variations: Gabriela, Gabriella, Gabrielle, Gab, Gabby

This name is not often given to boys these days, but its feminine forms are still quite popular. Perhaps people are more inclined to think of girls as "angels," but that's not a very biblical idea! Gabriel was the name of one of the archangels. We read of him being sent to earth with messages for God's servants. He appeared to Daniel (see Dan 8) and later came to Zechariah to tell him about the conception of his son, who would grow up to be John the Baptist (see Luke 1:5-25). The most important message which Gabriel ever delivered was surely the one which he brought to Mary, that she would bear the Son of God (Luke 1:19, 26).

Gaius

Meaning: from the Latin, "I am glad"

This Latin name seems to have been a very common one in the Roman Empire. Four men called Gaius are mentioned in the New Testament. Two of them travelled with Paul, and two others were leading men in their churches.

A Gaius who travelled with the apostle Paul was caught up in the persecution that broke out against Christians when Paul was preaching in Ephesus (Acts 19). He and his companion Aristarchus were seized by a riotous mob and dragged to the theater. After several hours, during which the two of them were shouted at and threatened, they were eventually released. In those early days of the Christian faith, this Gaius was just one of the many who were prepared to give their lives for the sake of Jesus and the gospel message. Another Gaius probably had a group of Christians meeting in his house in Corinth. The apostle Paul stayed in his home and from there wrote his letter to the Romans (Rom 16:23).

This name would be unusual in this day and age, but it has a good sound to it, and it was the name of some brave and useful members of the early Christian church.

Gideon

Meaning: from the Hebrew, "hewer," or "smiter"

Gideon was one of Israel's Judges. In his time the Israelites were being oppressed by the Midianites, and Gideon led his army to a great victory over them. Israel had many men who were prepared to go to war following Gideon's lead. However, God was determined to show that any victory won by Israel was *God's* victory. So God directed Gideon to choose only a small band of three hundred men. They attacked the enemy by night, carrying torches hidden in clay jars. In the sudden noise and light, the Midianites were totally confused. They fought each other and finally fled. It was indeed God's victory (Judg 6–8).

Gideon was essentially a very timid man. He was appalled when the angel of God first suggested to him that he should go and save Israel from the Midianites. But God gave him a great victory. The people then wanted to make him king, but he refused this privilege, knowing that only God should be the king of the Israelites. In the Letter to the Hebrews in the New Testament, Gideon is mentioned as one of the heros of the faith who "through faith conquered kingdoms" (Heb 11:32).

Gideon would make a fine name for a boy, and it would remind the child that God can use even weak and timid people to achieve great things.

Gomer

Meaning: from the Hebrew, "to finish" or "to complete"

In the Bible this is the name of both a man and a woman. The man is mentioned in Gen 10:2-3. He was the grandson of Noah and the son of Japheth, and was born after the great flood. The woman called Gomer was married to the prophet Hosea who lived in the eighth century B.C.E. She was a prostitute who, in spite of Hosea's help and love, returned to prostitution during their marriage. The marriage of these two, prophet and prostitute, was used by God as a picture of God's relationship with Israel. God was the loving husband who kept trying to bring his adulterous wife back into his home and care for her and love her. Gomer, on the other hand, was like Israel, always looking for other husbands, or other (pagan) gods. The book of Hosea paints for us a picture of the deep love which God has for the people, even though they sin again and again. God's people are acting like prostitutes in selling themselves to other rulers and other gods.

Perhaps (since it means "complete") this name would be suitable for the baby whom you think (or hope!) will be the last addition to your family. However, bearing in mind the character of Hosea's wife, Gomer, you probably won't give this name to a daughter!

Grace

Meaning: undeserved favor, mercy, and love

Nowadays we tend to think of grace as a physical characteristic. But the word "grace" as used in the Bible has a spiritual meaning. It refers to the wonderful love of God towards humankind, which is quite undeserved by sinful human beings. From divine grace God sent the Son into the world to redeem us, and by divine grace God pours out blessings upon us (see, for example, Eph 2:8).

Hannah

Meaning: from the Hebrew, "favored" or "grace"

Variations: Hana, Hanna, Hani, Nan, Nancy. See also Anna

Hannah was a wonderfully faithful woman who loved God, and she became the mother of Samuel, one of the greatest prophets in Israel's history. She had married Elkanah, who loved her dearly. But to their great sorrow, Hannah had no children, while Elkanah's other wife, Penninah, had several. Every year the family went to worship and sacrifice at Shiloh, and one year Hannah went to the Tent of Meeting (also known as the Tabernacle) and prayed earnestly that God would give her a son. She promised that if God did as she asked, she, in turn, would give the boy back to serve God all his life. Eli, the priest, seeing her in distress, thought she was drunk, but on hearing her story, he blessed her (1 Sam 1:9-18).

In due course her prayer was answered and Samuel was born. His name means "asked of God." Hannah praised God in a wonderful song about God's sovereignty and great power. When Samuel was three, Hannah brought him back to Shiloh and gave him into Eli's care and supervision so that he could work in the Tent of Meeting. Hannah visited him each year, bringing him a new robe. Later Hannah had three more sons and two daughters.

Hannah was a woman of great faith in God, praying over her griefs and problems, praising God for God's answers, and keeping her vow, whatever the cost to herself. What a pleasant person she must have been too! We are told that at the annual feast, her husband gave her a double portion of meat "because he loved her."

Hezekiah

Meaning: from the Hebrew, "God has strengthened"

This really would be a strange name to give a boy these days, and perhaps he would be teased at school because of it. But the Hezekiah of the Bible was a fine king of Judah who led a great nationwide revival when he came to the throne at the age of twenty-five. Worship in the land of Judah had fallen on bad times. The priests and Levites were not doing their duties and previous kings had not encouraged them. Hezekiah had the Temple cleared out and got them all back to work. A great celebration of Passover was held which lasted a full fourteen days. Word of the return to faith in God quickly spread through Judah and even into the kingdom of Israel. People came from all over the land to worship in the Temple. Hezekiah lived in the eighth century B.C.E. when the Assyrians were trying to capture the whole region. A number of notable stories are told in the Bible of how he asked God for help to deal with these formidable enemies and how God came to his rescue (2 Chr 29–32).

Hope

"Hope" is not actually a person's name in the Bible, but it has often been used as a name over the years. In the Bible hope is a word which is full of meaning. The "Christian hope" can best be summarized as the definite promise that Christ will return again to this earth to bring salvation to all who have faith in him. In 1 Corinthians 13:13, that famous chapter on love, hope stands alongside faith and love, all of which endure even beyond the grave.

Usually these days this name is given to girls, although occasionally in the past boys were called Hope. In the Bible the apostle Peter points out that hope in God was one of the characteristics that made many holy women seem so very beautiful (1 Pet 3:5).

Immanuel

Meaning: from the Hebrew, "God with us"

Male variations: Emmanuel, Manuel, Manny, Manolo

Female variations: Emmanuelle, Immanuelle, Manuela

This wonderful name is used in Isaiah 7:14 and Matthew 1:23. In Isaiah it looked forward to the birth of a child who would especially remind the people of God's presence with them in a very difficult time of invasion and trouble. In the New Testament Matthew reminds the reader that the ultimate expression of God being with God's people was Jesus, for Jesus is indeed Immanuel, "God with us." The problem with this name is simply that you might be giving your child too much to live up to! Imitating Jesus is difficult enough, and some may think that to be given his name is perhaps too much. On the other hand, the name is a vivid reminder of the presence of God with God's people, and what more could a parent want than that their child will grow up being able to say, "God is with me"?

Ira

Meaning: from the Hebrew, "wakefulness"; in Arabic it can mean "stallion"

In the Bible a remarkable man named Ira is listed among King David's thirty mighty warriors. He was an army commander in charge of twenty-four thousand men (2 Sam 23:26). Another warrior in David's forces was also called Ira (2 Sam 23:38). Parents with pacifist beliefs would probably not consider this to be a suitable name for their baby boy!

Iram

Meaning: from the Hebrew, possibly from "city"

This man was a descendant of Esau and became a chief in the area of Edom (Gen 36:43). This is hardly a common name these days, but you may be brave enough to try it!

Isaac

Meaning: from the Hebrew, "he laughs"

Variations: Isaak, Yitsak

God promised Abraham and Sarah that they would have a son, but so many years passed that they were beyond child-bearing age. When God then told Sarah that within a year her baby would be born, she laughed aloud in disbelief. But the baby was born at the stated time, and so the laughter and delight became real, and Abraham called the baby "he laughs" (Gen 21:3).

In his early life Isaac had a memorable experience that you would not want your child to have to go through! God tested Abraham's faith by asking him to offer up Isaac, this long-awaited and so deeply loved son, as a sacrifice. Abraham and Isaac climbed up a hill together and built an altar on it. Then Abraham bound his son and laid him on the altar as a sacrifice. Abraham's faith (and no doubt the young Isaac's!) had been tested to the limit. But just before the sacrifice took place, God stopped Abraham and provided a nearby ram as the offering (Genesis 22).

When Sarah died and Isaac needed comfort, Abraham sent a servant to bring a wife for Isaac from Abraham's original home-land. He returned with Rebekah, who was actually a cousin. Isaac loved her as soon as he saw her. They married and later had twins, Jacob and Esau. For most of his life Isaac stayed within a small area, tending his flocks, growing crops, and industriously ensuring that the land was adequately watered. God had told Rebekah that the younger twin, Jacob, would be served by the older, and Rebekah did her best to ensure this. Jacob received the blessing of his father, but Esau vowed to kill him at the first opportunity, so Jacob had to flee. Isaac lived to see his son return, but Rebekah had died by then.

Isaac was, for the main part of his life, a quiet and happy man, enjoying his wife, his twin boys, and his work. What a contrast with the travels and experiences of his father Abraham and his son Jacob! Yet Isaac had a deep love and reverence for God, and he was one of the three people whose names were used as an identification of God—"the God of Abraham, Isaac, and Jacob."

Ishmael

Meaning: from the Hebrew, "God hears"

If you have prayed for a child for a long time, then this name, with its meaning, may be very special to you and very suitable for your baby boy. However, be warned! The most famous Ishmael in the Bible, the son of Abraham and his concubine Hagar, is described in less than flattering terms! Genesis says he was "a wild ass of a man with his hand against everyone, and everyone's hand against him" (Gen 16:12). Not quite an ideal role model for your son! However, there are other Ishmaels in the Bible who seem to have been rather better people. A couple of them served God faithfully (see 2 Chr 19:11; 23:1; Ezra 10:22).

Jacinth

Meaning: the name of a jewel, named after the hyacinth (a flower in a variety of blues); the jewel is red-yellow

Female variations: Hyacinth, Jacinta

Male variation: Jacinto

Jacinth is a jewel mentioned in the Bible, and today the word is sometimes used as a girl's name. It was one of the jewels on the breastplate worn by the high priest. These jewels represented the twelve tribes of Israel, held upon the priest's heart before God (Exod 28:19). When the apostle John describes his vision of the New Jerusalem in the book of Revelation, he talks of jacinths in the foundations of the city (Rev 21:20). This would be an unusual but attractive name for your baby daughter or son.

Jacob

Meaning: from the Hebrew, "supplanter"

Male variations: Jack, Jackie, Jaco, Jake, Jock, Cob, Cobby, Diego. See also "James"

Female variations: Jacoba, Jacqueline, Jackie. See also "James"

Jacob was one of the great patriarchs of Israelite history. The grandson of Abraham and the son of Isaac (Gen 25), he was the twin of Esau. Although Esau had been born first, God had made it clear that it was through Jacob God's saving plan would progress. Instead of leaving things to God, Jacob deceived his father Isaac in order to get his blessing. Esau was so angry that Jacob fled to his uncle Laban. While with him, Jacob married Laban's two daughters, Leah and Rachel (Gen 29:16-30). Eventually he returned home and was somewhat reconciled to Esau.

Jacob had twelve sons and was the head of a large family, with flocks and herds. When famine came, he sent to Egypt for grain. He eventually discovered that his son Joseph had, without his knowledge, been sold by his brothers into Egypt as a slave and was now next in power to Pharaoh himself. Joseph obtained Pharaoh's permission for Jacob and all the family (seventy in all!) to come to live in Egypt. Jacob died in Egypt, but he had made Joseph promise that his body would be taken back to Canaan to be buried.

Jacob seems to have been a rather crafty, cunning person, but he also had great faith in God, and on many occasions God met with him to encourage and strengthen him. On one occasion Jacob saw a ladder going up to heaven with angels moving up and down on it. God used this to show Jacob that God would always be with him and would bless his descendants, the people of Israel (Genesis 28).

James

Meaning: an English version of Jacob

Male variations: Jaime, Jamie, Jim, Jimmy, Jimmie, Seamus

Female variation: Jamie. See also "Jacob"

Several men are called James in the New Testament. First, there is James the brother of Jesus, probably the next eldest in the family (Matt 13:55). From the record of the Gospels it would seem that he did not believe in Jesus as the Messiah until after the resurrection. However, he then soon became a leader in the church at Jerusalem. At the famous Council of Jerusalem (see Acts 15), his word was accepted with great respect by all present. At the end of Paul's third missionary journey, the apostle reported back to James in Jerusalem. He was probably the James who wrote the New Testament letter of that name.

Secondly, there was James the brother of John, both of whom were apostles. This James was a fisherman, working with his brother John, his father Zebedee, and also with Peter and Andrew. Jesus called all four of them to leave their fishing and to follow him. James with John and Peter were privileged to be with Jesus on several special occasions, such as the transfiguration (Matt 17) and the raising of Jairus' daughter (Mark 5). They were with Jesus for longer than the others in the Garden of Gethsemane at the end of his life (Matt 26). Very early in the life of the New Testament church, James was put to death for his faith. He was beheaded by King Agrippa (Acts 12:1-2). This James was a close friend of Jesus, but he had his faults as well! He and his brother John had quick tempers, and Jesus himself called them the "sons of Thunder" because of their desire to call down fire on a village which would not receive Jesus! James was also very ambitious, and was aware of his mother's request to Jesus that her two sons should have places of honor in Jesus' kingdom (Matt 20:20-23).

There was a third James among the apostles as well. He was known as James the son of Alphaeus. Mark refers to him as James the less, perhaps because he was the youngest James.

James was obviously a very popular name in the days of Jesus. These young Jewish babies would have been given the name in memory of the great patriarch Jacob. It has been the name of kings and great men down through the ages and is still a very popular name for boys and girls.

Jason

Meaning: **from the Greek for Joshua. Joshua means "God is salvation"**

Variation: Jay, Jas

Jason was a resident of Thessalonica. He made his home a center for the Christians in the town. On their travels Paul and Silas came to Thessalonica and Paul preached in the synagogue. Some of the Jews and many of the God-fearing Greeks believed his message and became Christians (Acts 17:4). This enraged some of the Jews and they tried to start a riot. Thinking that Paul and Silas would be there, they rushed to Jason's house. When they did not find them there, they dragged out Jason and some of the other Christians and brought them to face the city officials. They were charged with being "trouble-makers" and with worshiping a new king called Jesus. They were put on bail and released. Later that day Paul and Silas left the town.

Jason would be an excellent name for any baby boy. What a challenge for your child to live up to! Jason, like so many of the early Christians, showed great bravery. He had only recently become a Christian, and yet he was prepared to be persecuted and imprisoned for his faith.

Jasper

Meaning: **the name probably comes from the Persian meaning "master of the treasure." It can be many different colors and refers especially to a beautiful stone of reddish opaque quartz.**

Variations: Jaspar, Caspar, Kaspar—the proverbial name of one of the Wise Men who visited the baby Jesus (Matt 2)

In the Bible the word "jasper" is the name of a precious stone. A jasper was among the twelve jewels set in the breastplate of the high priest. These jewels represented the twelve tribes of Israel, held upon the priest's heart before God (Exod 28:20). When the apostle John tries to describe his vision of the New Jerusalem in the book of Revelation, he talks of jaspers in the foundations of the city (Rev 21:19). The city had a shining brilliance, "like jasper, clear as crystal." The biblical significance of jasper gives this boy's name a beautiful depth of meaning.

Jehu

Meaning: from the Hebrew, "the Lord is God"

This name is hardly ever used these days, so it would be unusual and would no doubt puzzle some people, but it has a lovely meaning. Several people in the Bible were called by this name. The most famous was "Jehu son of Nimshi," who was the tenth king of Israel and reigned for twenty-eight years (842–814 B.C.E.). Jehu had earlier been an army commander, but at God's instigation, a young prophet who followed Elisha anointed him to be king (1 Kgs 19:16-17). Jehu began his reign by seeking to serve the Lord, and he put to death the false prophets and some of the pagan aristocracy. However, he soon turned away from God (2 Kgs 10:31), and so God's judgment came upon the nation and the Assyrians took control of an ever-increasing area of the kingdom.

Jemimah

Meaning: from a Semitic word for "dove"

Variations: Jemima, Jemma, Jem, Yemima

Jemimah was a very beautiful woman mentioned in the Old Testament. Her father Job had known very great hardship during his life. He lost his animals, his servants, and even his family in one disaster after another. But towards the end of his life God again blessed him with even greater prosperity than he had originally possessed. His greatest blessing was a new family. He had seven sons and three daughters, of whom Jemima was the eldest. All the women were notably beautiful, and they all shared the family inheritance with their brothers (Job 42:12-15).

Jemima must have been beautiful, intelligent, and responsible. A good example for your little daughter!

Jeremiah

Meaning: possibly from the Hebrew, "*Yahweh** exults" or "*Yahweh* is exalted." Whatever the case, it is a name of praise to the God of Israel

Variations: Dermott, Diarmid, Jeremy, Jerry, Gerry, Jerram

Any growing lad could be proud of a name like this! Though several people in the Old Testament bore the name, the best known is Jeremiah the prophet. The son of a priest, he was born in a small village near Jerusalem. When he was still quite young, God called him to be a prophet. He prophesied for about forty years, telling the people that judgment would come on them because they had turned away from God and were disobeying God's commands. Jerusalem would be overthrown and completely destroyed, and the people would be taken into captivity. Because his prophecy was so unacceptable, he met with much opposition, and when Jerusalem was finally conquered, he narrowly escaped being put to death by his own people.

The nickname "Jeremiah" used to be given to people who were always gloomy and pessimistic, but this was most unfair to the biblical Jeremiah. He certainly had a message of destruction and woe, but there is also evidence that he was a very sensitive person. He had times of depression and almost despair at having such a hard message to preach and knowing that the people hated him for what he had to tell them, and yet he courageously continued.

A brave, sensitive man, Jeremiah faithfully carried out the difficult and thankless task that God had given him. He loved his people, the Israelites, very much and longed to see them turn in repentance to their God. In the modern form of "Jeremy" this would make a fine name for your son. (See the book of Jeremiah.)

*Yahweh is God's name revealed to Moses at the burning bush.

Jerusha

Meaning: from the Hebrew, "inheritance"

This name has not been in common usage in recent times, though it was used in England in the seventeenth century. In the Bible, Jerusha was the mother of King Jotham of Judah, and no doubt it was largely to her credit that Jotham grew up to love God and to do "what was right in the eyes of the Lord" (2 Kgs 15:33-34). Though unusual today, Jerusha would still make a beautiful name for a girl.

Jesse

Meaning: from the Hebrew, "God exists"

Male variation: Jess

Female variations: Jess, Jessamine, Jessica, Jessie

Jesse was a sheep farmer outside Bethlehem. He had eight sons, of whom David was the youngest. The prophet Samuel came to Jesse's house to anoint one of his sons as the next King of Israel, and to Jesse's astonishment it was David whom God had chosen (see 1 Sam 16). Later Jesse had to agree to allow David to serve King Saul as a harp player. In 1 Samuel 17 we read that Jesse sent David to see his brothers in the army and to take them some food. It was there that David heard the giant Goliath's challenge to the Israelites to send a man to fight him. David responded to the challenge, and killed the giant with a stone from his sling.

As the father of David, Jesse was an ancestor of Jesus and is mentioned in connection with David and Jesus on a number of occasions.

Jethro

Meaning: from the Hebrew, "excellence"

Variation: Jeth

Jethro was the father-in-law of Moses. After killing an Egyptian, Moses fled into the wilderness. There he became a friend of Jethro's family, and eventually he married Jethro's daughter Zipporah (Exod 2). When the Israelites had escaped from Egypt and were camping in the wilderness, Jethro visited Moses. He was concerned that Moses was overburdened with work and responsibility, so he suggested that Moses should delegate some of the judicial matters to capable helpers (Exod 18). Jethro was a kindly and wise man who recognized that God had done great things for Israel. This name sounds a little old-fashioned, but Jethro would make a worthy role model for a boy.

Jezebel

Meaning: from the Hebrew, possibly "divine prince"

Queen Jezebel was the wicked wife of King Ahab of Israel. She worshiped pagan gods and was renowned for her murderous persecution of those who trusted in the true God (1 Kgs 18–21). Very few parents would want to name their daughter after such an evil woman!

Joanna

Meaning: from the Hebrew, "God is gracious"

Variations: Joanne, Joni, Joan, Jane, Jean, Siobhan, Janet, Janice, Jane, Janine

Joanna was the wife of Chuza, the manager of King Herod's household. She was one of a group of women who had been healed by Jesus and who helped to provide for Jesus and his disciples out of their own means (Luke 8:2-3).

Joanna was with Jesus in Jerusalem at the end of his life. She may have helped to lay his body in the tomb after the crucifixion, and she was certainly one of the women who came back on the third day and was told that Jesus had been raised from the dead. She, with the others, rushed off to tell the disciples the wonderful news (Luke 24:9-10).

Job

Meaning: from the Hebrew, "hated" or "persecuted"

This man lived through some terrible sufferings and hardships in which he lost most of his possessions and his family died. However, he remained faithful to God throughout all this. He struggled with what he was going through as much as anyone would, but he still relied on God. Some of his so-called friends tried to persuade him that it was his sin which had brought all these troubles upon him, but Job knew that could not be the case because he was a just and righteous person. In fact, the source of Job's troubles was Satan himself. Satan was seeking to prove to God that even someone as faithful as Job could eventually turn against God if enough evil happened to him.

At the end of his dreadful ordeal, Job had still remained faithful, and God restored him to his former prosperity. Although Job is a name associated with quiet suffering, it is perhaps much better to remember the man's amazing faithfulness to God in all situations. (See the whole of the book of Job.)

Joel

Meaning: from the Hebrew, "the Lord is God"

Male variation: Jo

Female variation: Joelle

Several men in the Old Testament had the name Joel, but the best known is the prophet Joel, who wrote the book of that name around 800 B.C.E. He lived in the kingdom of Judah and warned his people about the judgment that was going to come on them from God. He spoke of the "day of the Lord," when evil would be judged and conquered. But afterwards there would be a time of peace when God's Spirit would be poured out on the people (Joel 2:28-32). The apostle Peter tells us in Acts 2:16-21 that this prophecy was fulfilled by the coming of the Holy Spirit on the day of Pentecost.

Being named after the prophet Joel might encourage a boy or girl to be faithful to God, even when it means saying difficult things and being unpopular with friends.

John

Meaning: from the Hebrew, "God is gracious"

Variations: Juan, Jack, Johnny, Ian, Sean, Owen, Evan, Jan

Name your child John, and he will have a lot to live up to, and you will have some wonderful stories to tell him about other people named John who lived in biblical times. There are four Johns in the Bible, but two are especially famous. The first is John the Baptist, whose story is told in the Gospels, especially Luke 1–3 and John 1:19-34. This John was born just before Jesus and became the last prophet. His God-given role was to prepare the people of Israel for the arrival of Jesus. He baptized people in the river Jordan as a sign of their repentance and their desire to return to serving God. His mother was too old to have children, and yet God miraculously gave her John. He was brave and faithful to God throughout his life. When Jesus began his public ministry, John was prepared to take second place to him. He stood up against Herod Antipas, warning him that God would judge him for his sins, so Herod had John thrown into prison, and eventually he was beheaded (Matt 14:3-12).

The second John is, of course, the apostle. He was the son of Zebedee and was almost certainly the one referred to in John's Gospel as "the disciple whom Jesus loved" (John 13:23). He had been a fisherman when Jesus first called him to be a disciple. Jesus gave him the nickname "Boanerges" ("son of thunder"), which suggests that he had quite a fiery temperament (Mark 3:17).

A deep personal friendship developed between Jesus and John. Later John wrote a Gospel and three letters which today are part of the New Testament. Led by the Holy Spirit, he was determined that later generations should know who Jesus was and is, and he longed for everyone to have faith in Christ as their Savior (John 20:31).

Jonah

Meaning: from the Hebrew, "dove"

Most people know Jonah as the man who survived being swallowed by a whale (actually it was a "large fish"). He was a prophet who was told by God to go to the great pagan city of Nineveh to tell the people there that God was going to destroy them because of their wicked ways. He did not want to go and, in fact, set off in a ship going in the opposite direction. When a great storm arose, Jonah confessed to the sailors that it was his presence on board which was endangering their lives, and he told them to throw him overboard.

Reluctantly, they did as he said, and the storm passed away. Jonah was swallowed by a great fish, and three days later he was cast up again on the shore. He then went to Nineveh. When the people heard his message, they believed it, repented of their evil ways, and turned to God. Jonah was very upset—he wanted God to punish them! He could not understand how *his* God could save people from other countries who were not Israelites. He had a lot to learn! God is prepared to forgive all people who repent, no matter what nation they come from. (See the book of Jonah in the Old Testament.)

If you call your son by this name, let's hope he doesn't get swallowed up by a big fish! Let's also pray that he will be able to talk about God when the situation arises and not run off in the other direction!

Jonathan

Meaning: from the Hebrew, "God has given"

Variations: Jonny, Jonnie, Johnathan, Jon

There are no fewer than fifteen men called Jonathan in the Old Testament, but the best known is the son of King Saul. Although he knew that after the death of his father, he would not be king himself (for God had appointed David to be the next king), he had a close friendship with David. When his father became jealous of David and tried to kill him, Jonathan warned David and helped him to flee. Jonathan was a brave commander in Saul's army. When he and his father were eventually killed in battle, David grieved greatly for him. Jonathan was a godly, brave man and a faithful, loyal friend. (See 1 Sam 13–14).

A baby boy is a gift from God, so this would make a fine name for him. It would be even more appropriate if he had a brother called David!

Joseph

Meaning: from the Hebrew, "God increases" or "may God add"

Male variations: Jo, Joe, Joey, José, Pepe

Female variations: Josepha, Josephine, Josie, Josey, Jodie, Pepita

This has always been a popular name. The best-known Joseph in the Bible was the husband of Mary, the mother of Jesus. He was a carpenter in Nazareth, and he was obviously a man who loved God deeply. He was chosen to be the head of the household in which the young Jesus would be cared for. A kindly, loving man, he was anxious to do what was best for Mary when he knew she was expecting a baby. After Jesus' birth, he was scrupulous in bringing the baby to the Temple and offering the sacrifices required for an eldest son. Each year he took the family to Jerusalem for the Passover. (See Matt 1–2; Luke 2:21-52).

There is also a Joseph in the Old Testament, and he too was a godly man. He was the eleventh son of Jacob. Having been sold into slavery by his brothers, he eventually rose to a position in Egypt second only to Pharaoh. When a great famine arose, Joseph had already made plans to store food, and so was able to sell it. His brothers came down to Egypt from Canaan to buy food, and Joseph was very moved to see them all again. Joseph soon made himself known to them and was able to keep them well supplied with food. Eventually he obtained Pharaoh's permission for the whole family to come to Egypt to live. Joseph always attributed all that happened to him, good or bad, to the hand of God. God used him to preserve the chosen people through the famine years. (See Gen 37–50).

If you give your child this name, he or she will have two good examples to follow, because both of the biblical Josephs were kindly men who were always willing to obey God.

Joshua

Meaning: from the Hebrew, "God is salvation"

Variations: Hoshea, Josh

Few people in the Bible can have had such an exciting and testing life as Joshua. Name your boy Joshua, and you will be opening up to him one of the most exciting periods in Israel's history, full of battles, of faith in God in almost impossible circumstances, and of stories which show God's care for the people.

When he was young, Joshua was close to Moses when the Israelites were journeying in the desert. It was Moses who changed the young man's name from Hoshea to Joshua (Num 13:16). Joshua became a fine soldier and warrior. He was present when Moses went up Mount Sinai. Also he was sent as one of the spies into Canaan when the chosen people reached the borders of the land. He and Caleb were the only two who brought back the report that, with God's help, the Israelites could conquer the land (Num 14:5-9). Their report was not accepted by the people, and for forty years the tribes remained in the desert. When Moses died, Joshua took over as the leader, and he led the armies in many successful battles during the conquest of Canaan (see the book of Joshua). Always he encouraged the people to follow and obey God. God repeatedly said to Joshua, "be strong and courageous" (Josh 1), and Joshua certainly followed this advice. His one aim was to carry out God's instructions, and he saw God work in wonderful ways. At the end of his life he declared that all of God's promises had come true.

Josiah

Meaning: from the Hebrew, "the God supports him"

Male variations: Jo, Joe (also see Joseph)

Female variation: Josie

The most famous Josiah in the Bible became king of Judah in 640 B.C.E. and reigned for around thirty years. He lived in difficult political times, when Egypt and Assyria were vying for power and poor Judah found itself stuck in the middle. He turned to God for help, and "did what was right in the sight of the Lord" (2 Kgs 22:2). During his reign, an amazing spiritual revival took place in the nation. Leading from the front, he threw out idols and pagan altars from the Temple and from the whole country. The Book of the Law (no doubt a version of the laws of God given to Moses) was discovered and read publicly. Josiah wanted to obey God's word, and so he listened intently and ensured that he and the priests and the people did all that God had commanded. There was a great celebration of the Passover in the Temple and in Jerusalem, and the people repented and were forgiven.

Josiah's love for the word of God and his desire to obey God led him and his country into a time of great blessing from God. This would be an unusual name for your child, but King Josiah would make a marvellous role model for him or her.

Joy

This is a lovely name which reflects one of the great themes running through the Bible. The word "joy" occurs well over two hundred times, and it usually describes the way people react to the goodness of God. In the Bible we see that God looks after people, and they are filled with joy because God loves and cares for them. In 1 Chronicles 16:25-27 we read: "For great is the Lord and greatly to be praised . . . Honor and majesty are before him; strength and joy are in his place." Then in the New Testament we often read of the joy which people feel when they come to believe in and know the Lord Jesus. The apostle Peter writes: "Although you have not seen him, you love him; and even though you do not see him now, you believe in him and rejoice with an indescribable and glorious joy" (1 Pet 1:8). This is clearly a kind of happiness that goes deeper than the external circumstances of our lives. Even in trouble, it is possible to feel joy.

If you give this name to your baby girl, it may help her to grow up with real joy in her heart.

Jude

Meaning: a variation of Judah, "praise"

Male variations: Jud, Judd

Female variations: See Judith

This would be an interesting name for a boy and it would be a reminder of the deep faith of those early Christians, who endured so much persecution. Jude, who wrote a letter in the New Testament, was probably the half-brother of Jesus, and it is likely that they grew up together. Perhaps like Jesus' other brothers, he came to believe in him as the Christ only towards the end of Jesus' life. Jude wrote his letter to encourage Christians to persist in their faith and to remind them that God knew all about their problems and could keep them from falling.

Judith

Meaning: from the Hebrew, "praise"

Variations: Jude (female form), Judi, Judy, Jody, Jodie

Judith is a very attractive name that has been popular for many years. In the Bible, Judith was the wife of Esau. Esau's parents, Isaac and Rebekah, were unhappy about the marriage, as Judith came from one of the heathen tribes living nearby (Gen 26:34).

The Judith in the Greek version of the Old Testament is better known. She was a widow, a devout worshiper of God, and she was very rich and beautiful. When the king of Assyria sent his general Holofernes to conquer Judea and the army was besieging Bethulia, Judith's town, the citizens finally wanted to surrender. But Judith persuaded them to wait and to let her try to save them. Judith prayed to God, put off her widow's clothes, and dressed in splendid garments. Then she and her maid went to the Assyrian camp. Holofernes was struck by her beauty and hoped to possess her. Judith got him drunk and cut off his head, which she and her maid took back to Bethulia. The Assyrian army fled in panic, and Judith sang a song of victory and praise to God.

Judith was a great heroine, and this is a name to give your daughter if you want her to be brave and always to call upon God to help her no matter how afraid she may be and whatever difficulty or even danger she may face.

Julia

Meaning: the feminine form of the Latin name Julius which may mean "fair-skinned"

Female variations: Jill, Juliet, Juliette, Julie, Juliana, Gill, Gillian

Male variations: Julius, Julian, Julio, Gillean

Many committed Christian women are mentioned in the New Testament. Some of them had small churches meeting in their houses. Others were wealthy business women or were simply renowned for their faith. The apostle Paul sent greetings to a number of them by name. Julia was a Christian woman living in Rome whom he mentions in Romans 16:15. We can deduce from this that she played an active part in the fledgling church there despite the risks that came with being a Christian in those days.

Justus

Meaning: from the Latin, "just"

Male variation: Justin

Female variations: Justina, Justine

The New Testament tells us of a man called Justus who was one of the two men who were considered by the apostles as a replacement for Judas, the disciple who betrayed Jesus and then committed suicide. (In the end, the other of the two men, Matthias, was chosen.) Justus could witness to the resurrection and was a good and devout man (Acts 1:21-23). Another man named Titius Justus is mentioned in Acts 18:7. He lived in Corinth and allowed the apostle Paul to use his home as a base.

Loyalty, integrity, and generosity are qualities which these two men shared, so they set an admirable example for your son or daughter to follow.

L

Leah

Meaning: from the Hebrew, "to be weary"

Variations: Lee, Lea, Leigh

Leah was the elder daughter of Laban, Jacob's uncle. Jacob fell in love with Laban's younger daughter Rachel, and worked for Laban for seven years in order to be allowed to marry her. After the wedding, during which the bride was completely veiled, Jacob found that he had been tricked and had been given Leah instead. He then worked for another seven years to be allowed to marry Rachel as well.

Leah had a lot of sadness in her life, so she was appropriately named. She was not as beautiful as her sister and she knew that her husband never loved her as much as he did Rachel. But God knew all her sorrow and blessed her with six sons. This gave Leah great status since, for a long time, Rachel had no children. All the boys had names which showed Leah's gratitude to God for her family, and she must have found happiness in her children.

This is an attractive name, but if you give it to your daughter, you might want to pray that her life will not be as sad as her name-sake's was!

Levi

Meaning: from the Hebrew, possibly "to pledge"

Levi was the third son of Jacob (Gen 29:34), and rather poignantly, he was given his name by his mother Leah, who had felt unwanted by her husband Jacob. We are told she gave the name saying, "Now this time my husband will be joined to me." Levi was infamous for the terrible revenge he took on the people of Shechem, the son of whose ruler had raped his sister (Gen 34). However, his descendants were later appointed priests for Israel.

Another famous man named Levi, better known as Matthew, appears in the New Testament. This man was a tax-collector for the Romans and was therefore considered disloyal and an outcast by the Jewish people. However, when Jesus came and spoke to him, Levi immediately followed Jesus and became one of the twelve apostles. Money had probably been the chief passion in his life, but when he met Jesus, a wonderful change happened to him.

Levi would be an unusual but fine name for a boy today.

Linus

Meaning: from the Latin, "flax"

Female variations: Linett, Linette, Lynnet, Lynette

In the Bible, Linus was a friend of the apostle Paul and of Timothy. He was probably one of those who visited Paul when he was imprisoned in Rome (2 Tim 4:21). This suggests that he was a caring, loving man, so he is a good example for any child named after Linus to follow.

Lois

Meaning: from the Greek, perhaps "desirable"

Most parents think their lovely new daughter is "desirable." It may not be a common name, but it certainly has a beautiful meaning, and it will help her to remember, as she grows up, how much you love her and think of her. In the Bible, Lois was the grandmother of Timothy (2 Tim 1:5). Lois and her daughter Eunice probably were Jews and became Christians when Paul first preached in

Lystra. Both mother and grandmother brought the boy up to share their faith and to know the Bible. When Paul returned to Lystra, he found that Timothy was a young man well fitted to travel with him and to take an important role in Christian ministry. Lois is a reminder to all mothers (and fathers) of how important and worthwhile it is to bring their children up to know the Bible and have faith in God.

Lucius

Meaning: from the Latin, "light-giving"

Male variations: Lucian, Lucien

Female variations: Lucy, Lucie, Luz, Lucinda, Lucille, Lucasta

This would be a rare but pleasing name to give a baby boy. Two people have this name in the New Testament. The first is Lucius of Cyrene, who was one of the "prophets and teachers" in the church at Antioch (Acts 13:1). Lucius may have been among those Jewish Christians from a Greek background who, having been scattered by persecution, came to Antioch and began to tell the Greek-speaking Jews there the good news about "the Lord Jesus" (Acts 11:20). So in spreading the "light" of the gospel message Lucius was living up to the meaning of his name!

The second Lucius was either a fellow Jew or a blood relative of Paul and was one of those who were with the apostle when he wrote his letter to the Roman church (Rom 16:21).

Perhaps the name and the example of Lucius of Cyrene will help your son or daughter to grow up to give out the light of the gospel to the world.

Luke

Meaning: from the Latin, "of Lucania"

Male variations: Lucas, Luck

Would you like your child to grow up to be a caring, faithful doctor, always ready to stand up for his friends, and perhaps even a writer as well? Then perhaps you should think of this name! In the New Testament Luke was a Greek doctor and a friend of the apostle Paul, travelling with him on several missionary journeys. Paul refers to him as "Luke, the beloved physician" (Col 4:14). Paul was particularly appreciative that Luke was the only friend with him in Rome during his trial before the emperor.

Luke wrote two books of the New Testament: the Gospel of Luke and the Acts of the Apostles. He wanted to write an orderly account of Jesus' life and the early church and to establish their historicity. He interviewed many eye-witnesses and so produced his two remarkable books. He produced pen-pictures of many people in all walks of life, and he wrote with great empathy. He also wrote down many hymns and songs for future generations (the best known is "Mary's Song," often called the *Magnificat*). He also recorded some of Jesus' parables for us, including some which are not recounted in the other Gospels. His great emphasis was that the message of the gospel, of Jesus as Savior, was for everyone. Luke was an outstanding person. He was a physician, an inspired writer, and a faithful friend. Any boy should feel proud to be given his name.

Lydia

Meaning: from the Greek, "a woman of Lydia," a kingdom which once extended over most of Asia Minor (modern Turkey)

Variations: Liddie, Lidia, Lydda

Giving your daughter the name Lydia may set her on the right track to become a godly, honest, and successful business-woman. That is how the New Testament describes Lydia, who met the apostle Paul in Philippi (see Acts 16:14). She had moved there from Thyatira, and her trade was in selling purple-dyed cloth. The use of purple suggests that her business was with wealthy people and that she was rich. But that was just one side of her life, for she also used to meet with other women down by the river bank to pray and to worship God. When Paul joined them and told them about Jesus Christ, she believed his message, and Paul baptized her and her household. She then invited him to stay in her home.

Lydia is a fine example of many Greek women in the cities which Paul visited. Often they were successful business-women who worshipped the God of the Jews. When they became Christians, they then became deeply involved in the church and in spreading the gospel message. The Bible says that God opened Lydia's heart to believe. If you name your daughter Lydia, you may want to pray that God will do the same thing for her.

M

Magdalene

Meaning: from the Hebrew, "from Magdala"

Variations: Madeleine, Madeline, Madelon, Maddy, Maud, Maude, Magda, Lena

Mary Magdalene was one of the women who followed Jesus on his journey and used their own money to provide for him and the Twelve (Luke 8:2-3). Luke also says that Jesus had freed her from seven demons. She is not the woman who washed Jesus' feet with her tears (Luke 7:36-50). She was so grateful to Jesus, loved him so much, and believed his message of salvation so deeply that she never abandoned him, even when he hung on the cross.

In the Synoptic Gospels (Matthew, Mark, and Luke), it was Mary Magdalene and the other faithful women to whom the angels announced the resurrection. In John's Gospel, it was to her that Jesus first appeared, and he told her to go and announce his resurrection to the disciples. For this reason she has been called since early times "the apostle to the apostles."

Mary Magdalene was a woman who loved Jesus with all her heart and followed him faithfully, never counting the cost. She would be a splendid role model for your daughter.

Mark

Meaning: from the Latin, possibly "large hammer" and possibly derived from the name of the Roman god Mars

Male variations: Marc, Marcus, Mars

Female variations: Martina, Marcella, Marcia, Marcie, Marsha

Mars was the Roman god of war, so you may need to watch out for this one, and "large hammer" doesn't bode well either! Nevertheless, the biblical Mark was a kindly and gracious man. Mark helped the apostle Paul and Barnabas in their missionary work as they took the good news about Jesus far and wide around the Mediterranean world (Acts 12:25).

Mark and Paul did not always see eye to eye (Acts 15:36-38), but much later in his life, Paul said Mark had been a great comfort to him (Col 4:10-11). Mark was also very friendly with the apostle Peter so he moved in good company and proclaimed the message of the love of Jesus for all people. So, in spite of the meaning of his name, Mark provides a lovely picture of what your child may grow up to be!

Martha

Meaning: from the Aramaic, "lady"

Variations: Martie, Marty, Mardi, Marta, Matty

Martha lived with her sister Mary and her brother Lazarus in Bethany, a village near Jerusalem. This threesome were friends of Jesus, and sometimes he stayed in their home (John 11). Martha seems to have been the housekeeper. In fact, Jesus once gently rebuked her for being so busy preparing a meal that she had no time to talk to him! When Lazarus was ill, the sisters sent for Jesus. Though he delayed his coming so much that Lazarus had been dead for four days by the time he arrived, Jesus then raised

Lazarus to life. Martha, a woman of great faith, had taken the lead in meeting Jesus, expressing her total faith in him and leading him to the tomb. Rejoicing over Lazarus' recovery, Martha probably gave a supper party!

This would be a wonderful name to give your daughter. Perhaps she will grow up to be a busy home-maker who likes entertaining guests and who has a great love for the Lord Jesus and a real understanding of who he is.

Mary

Meaning: from "Miriam," possibly from the Egyptian, "beloved"

Female variations: Maria, Marianne, Marie, Marin, Marika, Maura, Maureen, Miriam, Moira, Marietta, Marilyn

Male variations: Mario, Marius

This is one of the most common girls' names, and yet it is no less beautiful for that. There are six Marys in the New Testament, but the one everyone immediately thinks of is, of course, Mary the mother of Jesus. Not many mothers would like to have their first baby in a stable (see Luke 2)! But it was typical of this brave woman that she was prepared to accept anything that came her way.

Her great desire was to serve God, and God had called her to serve in the most amazing manner: to be the mother of God's own Son, Jesus. The angel Gabriel had told her that God wanted her to be the mother of the long-awaited Savior of the world, and in spite of the fact that she had not been married at the time, she had accepted her calling. She probably suffered a certain amount of scorn for being pregnant and unmarried, but her fiancé Joseph stood by her and soon married her. If the birth of Jesus had been hard for her, it must have been almost unbearable for her to watch her wonderful son dying in such a horrific way on a cross. But she still remained faithful to God and was always willing to do God's will. She stands for all time as an example of a woman who was greatly blessed by God and who was prepared to serve God whatever the personal cost.

Matthew

Meaning: from the Aramaic, "gift of God"

Variations: Mat, Matt. See also Matthias

Matthew, also called Levi, had a very unpopular job. He was a tax-collector, taking money from the Jews to pay it over to the Romans, who ruled their country. He probably worked on the edge of Capernaum, where he would receive customs and excise duties on goods coming by boat across the Sea of Galilee. Jesus saw Matthew sitting in his tax booth and called him to follow him, which Matthew immediately did. He then gave a feast for all his friends and fellow-workers so that they could meet Jesus (Matt 9:9).

The Jewish leaders considered tax-collectors to be the lowest people in society, and they were angry that this man Jesus was willing to mix with them. Jesus replied that even tax-collectors were people who needed him. It is probable that it was Matthew who went on later to write one of the four gospels.

This is a fine name for a boy, and perhaps it would encourage your son to follow Jesus, as Matthew did, and to introduce him to his friends!

Matthias

Meaning: from the Aramaic, "gift of God"

Variations: Mat. See also Matthew

All children are a "gift" from God, and this name will help you to remember this. Sometimes we forget this truth—for example, when we are woken up several times in one night!

In the Bible, Matthias was appointed by the other disciples to take Judas' place after the tragedy in which Judas, who had betrayed Jesus, had killed himself. The apostles gathered together to discuss the matter and, after much prayer, Matthias was chosen

(Acts 1:23-26). We know that he had been with the original twelve disciples right through the Lord's ministry and that he must have seen Jesus after he rose from the dead.

Michael

Meaning: from the Hebrew, "who is like God"

Male variations: Mick, Mickie, Micky, Miguel, Mike, Misha

Female variations: Michelle, Michaela, Michal, Mickie, Micheline

There are several men in the Old Testament called Michael: the father of one of the spies sent by Moses into Canaan; one of those who returned to Jerusalem with Ezra; the leader of a clan of Gaddites, and others. The best-known Michael is probably the archangel of that name. While the angel Gabriel was the messenger, Michael was a warrior fighting against Satan's forces on behalf of the people of God. In a vision Daniel saw Michael protecting all of God's people so that God's purposes for them would be worked out (Dan 12:1). In the book of Revelation, John saw him fighting against Satan in heaven, and throwing him down to earth so that he could no longer accuse God's people (Rev 12:7).

Michael has always been a popular name, and no wonder. After all, what little baby isn't also a "little angel"! Having the same name as an angel who defends and protects God's people would be exciting for any growing boy or girl, and it would give their parents plenty of opportunity to explain to them that God wonderfully protects and cares for all who have faith.

Michal

Meaning: from the Hebrew, "who is like God" (a shortened form of Michael)

Variations: Michaela, Michelle

We don't often think of this as a girl's name, the masculine form of the name being much more familiar to us. In the Bible, Michal was King Saul's younger daughter. With her father's reluctant permission she married David (1 Sam 17–18), and she saved his life when Saul planned to kill him (1 Sam 19). But their relationship was not successful, and it was not made any easier by the fact that David was often away at war. She despised him when he worshiped God by dancing in the streets, since she felt that this was not appropriate behavior for a king (2 Samuel 6). David rebuked her, and the rest of her life seems to have been rather sad and perhaps quite lonely. She died without children.

Miriam

Meaning: possibly from the Egyptian, "beloved"

Many children like to look after babies, but few girls are given as much responsibility as Miriam's mother gave her. Miriam was the elder sister of Moses, and her mother gave her the job of watching over her baby brother in his cradle among the bulrushes in the Nile. By order of the Pharaoh, the Hebrew boy babies had to be killed, but Moses' mother tried to save him. As Miriam watched, an Egyptian princess came along, saw the cradle, and decided to take the baby home. Miriam stepped forward to suggest her mother as a nurse for the child (Exod 2).

Years later, as the Israelites left Egypt and travelled in the desert, Miriam is described as a prophetess. God may have given messages through her, but when she and Aaron, her other brother, became jealous and challenged Moses' authority, God made it perfectly clear that is was Moses who was the divinely chosen leader.

Miriam was a leader among the Israelites, someone used to responsibility from an early age. She would be a fine role model for anyone's daughter.

Mishael

Meaning: from the Hebrew, "who is what God is" (pronounced "Meeshael")

One of the strongest messages of the Bible is that there is nothing and no one greater than God, and this name, rather like the names Michael and Michal, expresses that great truth. Though this name is undoubtedly unusual in the English-speaking world, it is used elsewhere and is worth considering for a young son. It sounds pleasant and will remain a firm reminder to him of the greatness and love of God.

In the Bible there are three people with this name. Two were probably priests or Levites and the other was one of the three friends of Daniel who were thrown into the fiery furnace when they refused to say that the Babylonian king Nebuchadnezzar was like God. Mishael stood true to his name and he and his two friends were eventually rescued from the fire by God's miraculous intervention (Daniel 3).

Mordecai

Meaning: from the name of the Babylonian god Marduk

Variations: Mortie, Morty

We would all like to have a son who would be fiercely loyal to his family and friends and prepared to risk his life for them and who would be truthful and honest in business. This was the sort of person Mordecai was. His story is told in the book of Esther. An exiled Jew living in Persia, he excelled in the service of King Xerxes and became a senior official in the government. He encouraged his cousin, Esther, to take advantage of her position as the queen so that she was able to speak to Xerxes on behalf of the Jewish people when a fierce outbreak of anti-Semitism erupted. The king allowed the Jews to defend themselves, and so they were saved from destruction. At great personal risk to himself, Mordecai remained faithful to his people and his God.

Moses

Meaning: from the Hebrew, "drawn out of the water"

Your child may not grow up in a royal court, but he will be sure to do well if you love him as much as Moses' mother, Jochebed, loved her little baby. The story of Moses is well known (see the book of Exodus, especially chapters 1–3). The Egyptians were killing all the male children born to the Israelites and were forcing the rest of the people to work in slavery. When Moses was born, his mother put him in a little reed basket that she floated among the bulrushes at the side of the river Nile. She sent Moses' older sister, Miriam, to keep watch on the basket and to make sure no one stole the baby. One of Pharaoh's daughters came to the river to bathe, found the baby, and realizing he was a young Israelite, decided to take him home and look after him in the royal court. Miriam ran up to her and suggested that she could find the princess a wet-nurse for the baby. She accepted the offer, so Miriam went to fetch the baby's own mother! Moses was then brought up in the Egyptian court. Years later, after God had made him the leader of the Israelites, he came back to the court to plead for the release of his people from their captivity.

Eventually, after God's judgment came upon them, the Egyptians did let Moses lead the people out of Egypt, across the Red Sea, and on towards the land of Canaan, which God had promised would one day be theirs. Moses became the greatest leader of the Israelites and was directly led by God. God gave him the Law and even counted him as a "friend." Moses had very low self-esteem, but no matter how often he felt he couldn't do what God was asking of him, God enabled him to do the job at hand. He provides us with a wonderful model of a man who had many faults but was ultimately prepared to go where God wanted him to go, and to do jobs for God for which he felt he was ill-equipped.

N

Naomi

Meaning: from the Hebrew, "pleasant," "charming"

Hopefully, giving this name to your baby girl will encourage her to be like her namesake! Naomi was a charming woman who, even through sad and tragic times in her life, remained faithful to God and was prepared to leave her life in God's hands.

During a famine in Judah, Naomi and her husband went to live in Moab. Their two sons married Moabite women, Ruth and Orpah. After some years, both her husband and her two sons died, and Naomi decided to go back to Judah. In very moving words, her daughter-in-law Ruth insisted that she would go with her. So they went to Judah together. While working in the fields there to get food, Ruth met a man named Boaz. He was a relative of Naomi, and eventually, following the custom of those days, Boaz married Ruth and redeemed the land which had previously belonged to Naomi's husband. Their baby, Obed, who was an ancestor of Jesus, was a great joy to Naomi. (For the story of Naomi see the book of Ruth.)

Nathan

Meaning: from the Hebrew, "a gift"

Variations: Nat, Nate. See also Nathaniel

Most parents feel that their child is a gift from God, and what better name than this to acknowledge that fact. The biblical Nathan was a prophet. King David had built himself a palace. After doing this, he wanted to build a temple for God, so he consulted Nathan. Nathan had to bring David the disappointing news that he was not to be the one to build the Temple. However, with this message, Nathan also brought David wonderful assurances of the love and blessing of God upon him and his family (2 Sam 7). At their next recorded meeting, Nathan had to speak to King David about the wickedness of his adultery with Bathsheba and about the punishment that God would bring upon him. At the end of his life, David called Nathan to anoint Solomon to be the next king.

Nathan remained loyal to David, but above all he was faithful to God, even when he had to take rather disturbing messages from God to the king.

Nathaniel

Meaning: **from the Hebrew, "God has given"**

Variations: See Nathan

This name is another wonderful reminder that all children are a "gift from God." In the New Testament Nathaniel came from Cana in Galilee and was one of Jesus' earliest disciples. Philip introduced him to Jesus, and Nathaniel was overawed to discover that Jesus seemed to know a great deal about him, and he was quick to acknowledge that Jesus must be the Son of God (John 1:49). Nathaniel is also listed among those who saw Jesus after the resurrection.

Nicholas

Meaning: from the Greek, "conqueror" for the people

Male variations: Nick, Nic, Nicky, Niki, Nikolas, Cole, Colin

Female variations: Nicole, Nickie, Nicky, Nicol, Nicola, Colette

This would be an excellent name for any boy or girl. Nicholas was one of the faithful and caring early Christians mentioned in the book of Acts (Acts 6:5). He had come from Antioch to Jerusalem and joined the church there, where he was quickly given a position of great responsibility.

Complaints had arisen in the church about the daily distribution of food to widows. Some had claimed that the Greek-speaking Jewish women were not treated equally with the Aramaic-speaking Jewish women. So the apostles told the community to appoint seven suitable men to serve as deacons to oversee the matter. These men had to be men of faith "filled with the Holy Spirit" (Acts 6:5). Nicholas was one of those selected, so we can be sure that he was well known in the church and was considered to be a very committed and mature Christian with a heart filled with God's love, joy, and peace. To be fit to do this difficult job, he would have been a caring and sensitive person as well as an honest, reliable, and truthful one.

Nicodemus

Meaning: from the Greek, "conqueror for the people"

Variations: Nic, Nick. See also Nicholas

This is not a particularly likely name for your boy, but it would be unusual and goes right back to the time of Jesus. Nicodemus came to speak with Jesus at night (see John 3). Perhaps this was for the sake of secrecy because Nicodemus was a Pharisee and probably didn't want his colleagues to know that he had gone to see Jesus.

Since he came to Jesus' defense when the chief priests and Pharisees were trying to condemn him, it is likely that he became a believer. After Jesus' death, Nicodemus came with Joseph of Arimathea to take away the body and prepare it for burial.

Noah

Meaning: from the Hebrew, "rest"

Surely Noah must be one character in the Bible of whom everyone has heard! He was a man who loved God and lived a good life in an age of great evil (Gen 6–8). God planned to destroy all the wickedness and evil in the great flood but told Noah to make a huge boat in which his family and representatives of all the animals could be kept safe. Noah must have been the subject of much ridicule and taunting since he probably spent years building the ark. But he remained faithful to God even though, at times, the whole idea must have seemed crazy! Eventually the great flood did come and Noah, together with his family and many animals, boarded the ark. When the flood had subsided, they all emerged on to dry land. Noah offered sacrifices to God, and God put a rainbow in the sky and promised that never again would a flood be sent to cover the whole earth.

If you name your son Noah, he may not become a shipbuilder, but you could pray that he will be as obedient and faithful to God as Noah was.

O

Olive

Meaning: a tree that is grown in Mediterranean climates and bears a fruit that gives a valuable oil

Variations: Olivia, Livia, Olivet, Olivette

This is not the name of a person in the Bible, but it is sometimes used as a name for girls these days, particularly in its common form of Olivia. Olive wreaths have been used as a mark of great honor, and olive oil is known to have great healing properties and was also used to provide light in small lampstands (Exod 27:20). From ancient times the olive has also been a symbol of peace, and fine olive oil became a synonym for all that was wonderful and good (Num 18:12). In the Bible the olive tree and its fruit are mentioned on numerous occasions.

Olive groves would have been a common sight throughout Old Testament and New Testament times. In Jesus' time such groves were to be found all across the area known as the Mount of Olives situated not far from the Temple in Jerusalem (Mark 11:1). An olive tree is even used as a symbol for God's people in Jer 11:16 and Rom 11:17-24.

Omar

Meaning: the early Hebrew meaning is not known, but in Arabic the name means "most high"

This name is quite common in the Arabic-speaking world today, but in the Bible only one person carried the name, and he was the grandson of Esau who became a leader among the people of Edom (Gen 36:15).

P

Patience

Nowadays this name sounds rather quaint, but what parent would not be thrilled to have a child called Patience who lived up to her name! We all need some patience in our lives. Patience is not actually a person's name in the Bible, but it has often been used as a name over the years. In the Bible patience is first and foremost a characteristic of God, who is repeatedly seen to be patient with people, even when they sin or disobey. Patience is also seen to be a fruit of the Holy Spirit. In other words, if people believe and trust in the God of the Bible and receive God's Holy Spirit, they may be expected to show something of this wonderful characteristic. They will be people who love and forgive because God loves and forgives them (Gal 5:22; Col 1:11; 3:12).

Paul

Meaning: **from the Latin,** *paulus* **or "little"**

Male variations: Pablo, Paolo, Pauly, Paulinus

Female variations: Paula, Pauline, Paulette

The apostle Paul was one of the greatest teachers the world has ever known. He grew up as a strict Pharisee but was converted to the Christian faith after a very dramatic vision on the road to Damascus. He was travelling from Jerusalem to Damascus with the aim of destroying the new group of Christians, but on the way he encountered a blinding light that knocked him to the ground (Acts 9). A voice spoke to Paul, asking him, "Saul, Saul, why do you persecute me?"(Saul was Paul's Hebrew name). Paul asked who was speaking and discovered that it was Jesus. This experience entirely changed Paul's life. From that moment on he began to preach about the love of God seen in Jesus and about how Jesus had died to bring forgiveness to people.

As he travelled widely around the whole Mediterranean area, taking this message with him, so people began to persecute him, and he was thrown into prison in a number of cities before finally coming to trial before the emperor in Rome.

Paul was an educated Jewish Pharisee who was also a Roman citizen. Thirteen letters in the New Testament are attributed to him. His teaching has really set the pace for what it is to be a Christian and how Christian people should live and behave. One of Paul's most significant contributions was the way he took the Christian message beyond the Jewish communities and made it available to people of all nations, provided they were prepared to have faith in Christ.

He stands as one of the great examples of faith for all time. In the end he was prepared to die for what he believed.

Pearl

Meaning: a precious jewel formed inside an oyster

When used as a girl's name, this word clearly expresses value and preciousness. In a world where people are often undervalued and put down, this name would be a lovely way of affirming the worth of your child. Jesus said the kingdom of heaven is like a pearl that is so valuable that it would be worth the sacrifice of everything else to obtain it (Matt 13:45). In the apostle John's description of the New Jerusalem the twelve gates of the city are each made of a pearl (Rev 21:21). Although this name is now less popular than it used to be, any girl named Pearl would love to be told how valuable pearls are and how they were considered so special even by Jesus.

Persis

Meaning: from the Greek, possibly "Persian"

Though this is not a common name by any means, it might be chosen by parents who hope and pray that their girl will grow up to work hard for the Lord Jesus. As the apostle Paul wrote letters to the various churches, he included greetings to particular people. Persis belonged to the church in Rome, and Paul called her "beloved." He remembered that she had worked very hard for the Lord (Rom 16:12).

Peter

Meaning: from the Greek, "rock"

Male variations: Pedro, Pieter, Pete, Pierce, Perry, Piers

Female variations: Petra, Pet, Petrina, Pierina, Piera

We all need a little excitement in our lives, and most children give their parents that—sometimes more than they really want! The apostle Peter must have been a bit like that, so if you use this name, you can look forward to some fun times and some frustrating times.

Peter was a kind but excitable person. He was the sort who could be the most committed of friends, and yet he could put his foot in it in the most frustrating ways. He was a fisherman on the Sea of Galilee when, one morning, Jesus came to speak to him. With characteristic impulsiveness, Peter listened to Jesus, left his boat, and spent the next three years with Jesus, travelling the country as one of twelve disciples who came to be called apostles.

Peter came to love Jesus very much and was hugely impressed by his message of love and forgiveness, and by the miracles that Jesus was performing. Peter was the first of the disciples clearly to identify Jesus as the Christ, the great king whom the Jews had been expecting God to send for many centuries (Mark 8:29). Yet, almost immediately after that, he put his foot in it by trying, with the best of intentions, to persuade Jesus that he should not go to Jerusalem, where he was bound to be killed. Jesus responded very strongly indeed to this statement, which would have led him away from following the will of God (Mark 8:33).

Peter was among Jesus' inner group of disciples, which included the brothers James and John, who were given the privilege of seeing Jesus appear in a glorified form with Moses and Elijah on the Mount of Transfiguration. But it was typical of Peter that at such a special time, when he should have been listening to the words of Jesus and of God, he blurted out, "Let us make three dwellings here"—as if such a moment could somehow be contained! (See Mark 9:2.)

It was Peter who, out of his love for and commitment to Jesus, proudly boasted that he was prepared to die for Jesus and would never forsake his master, only to be told by Jesus that in less than twelve hours' time he would have denied Jesus three times (John 13:37-38). After his betrayal Peter was full of remorse, and yet after the resurrection Jesus took him aside and quietly showed his forgiveness and encouraged him by saying to him, "Feed my sheep" (John 21:17).

This is what Peter went on to do, as he became one of the great Christian preachers and apostles of his generation. He took the Christian message even to non-Jewish people. He helped to lead the church in Jerusalem and wrote two letters that are now in the New Testament. It seems that eventually he gave his life for his faith.

Philip

Meaning: from the Greek, "lover of horses"

Male variations: Phil, Philly, Pip, Phillip, Felipe

Female variations: Philippa, Pip, Pippa, Phili

Loving horses can be an expensive business, so if you use this popular name for your boy or girl you will want to tell them more about their namesakes than about horses!

One of the twelve apostles was called Philip. Like Andrew and Peter, he lived in Bethsaida, and was called by Jesus to follow him. He brought Nathaniel to meet Jesus, assuring him that Jesus was the Messiah foretold by the prophets (John 1:44-47). His faith in Jesus grew slowly, though. When faced with feeding a crowd of five thousand, Jesus turned to Philip, but Philip could think only of the cost of buying food for so many (John 6:1-7). After the Last Supper he was anxious that Jesus should show them God the Father, and Jesus was disappointed that Philip had not grasped that he and the Father were one. This Philip is last heard of as being with the other disciples on the day of Pentecost (Acts 1:13).

Another Philip was a deacon and an evangelist. When the apostles needed help in distributing food to the poor and the widows, they chose seven men, including Philip, to be deacons to oversee the task. When persecution broke out in Jerusalem, Philip went to Samaria, where he had a successful preaching ministry and many people became Christians (Acts 8:12). Through the guidance of the Holy Spirit he went into the desert where he met an Ethiopian official. This man was reading from the book of Isaiah as he travelled back from Jerusalem. Philip explained the words of Isaiah to him and told him about Jesus. The Ethiopian believed and was baptized (Acts 8:27-39). In this way the gospel probably reached Ethiopia.

Phoebe

Meaning: from the Greek, "shining"

Every family is the better for having children who put others first, and this is just what Phoebe did in the New Testament. So perhaps giving this name to your daughter will encourage her to behave in this way. Phoebe belonged to the church in Cenchreae, a port city about seven miles east of Corinth. In Romans 16:1, the apostle Paul calls her a "deacon of the church," so it may be that she acted as a deaconess in the church. Paul clearly had a great regard for her work and said she had been a wonderful help to many people, including himself. She may have carried Paul's letter to Rome, for Paul asked the church there to give her any help she might need. We are given a picture of a godly woman who was an important member of the church, working hard for the Lord and obviously much loved.

Porcius

Meaning: probably from the Latin for "hog" or "pig"

Given that this word is perhaps where we get the word "pork" from and that this gives rise to all sorts of unhappy nicknames, you may feel this is not a suitable name for your child! In the Bible one Porcius is mentioned, and he was the Roman governor of Judea (see Acts 24:27). He was also called Festus.

Priscilla

Meaning: from the Latin, probably "ancient" or "old-fashioned"

Variations: Prisca, Scilla, Cilla, Prissie

In the New Testament the woman Priscilla is always mentioned together with her husband Aquila. They were dear friends of the apostle Paul and were busily engaged with work in the church during his ministry. They left Rome in C.E. 49, when an edict of Claudius expelled the Jews from the capital city. They travelled to Corinth, which the apostle Paul also visited (Acts 18). For a while he worked with them as a tentmaker, and also lived with the couple in their home.

Later Priscilla and Aquila went with Paul to Syria and then settled in Ephesus. Here they found a Jew named Apollos who was preaching about Jesus although he did not know the full story of the gospel. Priscilla and Aquila took him into their home and taught him more. A church even met in their home, which was where churches commonly met at that time.

Priscilla is shown as an intelligent and dynamic Christian woman, teaching the gospel with her husband and using her home in the Lord's service. She is a wonderful person to be named after.

R

Rachel

Meaning: from the Hebrew, "ewe"

Variations: Rachael, Raquel, Ray, Shelley

Rachel must have been beautiful and must have had a lovely character, for hers is one of the great love stories of the Bible. She was the younger daughter of Laban, the uncle of Jacob. Jacob fell head over heels in love with this beautiful woman when he was working for his uncle. So Jacob offered to continue working for Laban for seven years without wages if he could then have Rachel as his wife. He served the seven years, which "seemed to him but a few days because of the love he had for her" (Gen 29:20), and then a marriage ceremony took place. No doubt in those days the bride was veiled during the actual ceremony, for Jacob soon discovered that Laban had cheated him and had given him the elder daughter, Leah. Laban then agreed that Jacob could marry Rachel as well, if he worked a further seven years. Jacob's love for her was so great that he agreed to do this, and eventually they married.

Rachel later became distressed when her sister Leah had several children while she had none, but eventually she had a son, Joseph, and later a second child, Benjamin. Rachel died giving birth to him. She was buried near Bethlehem and, many years later, just before he died, Jacob spoke of his sorrow at her death. Rachel was a beautiful woman who was very deeply loved.

Raphael

Meaning: from the Hebrew, "God heals"

Female variation: Raphaella

If you would like your son or daughter to grow up to be a healer, a protector, a faithful companion, then this would be a good name for your baby.

Raphael is an archangel and one of the main characters in the book of Tobit, which is in the Greek version of the Old Testament, called the Septuagint. In that book, Tobit (or Tobias) is taken to Nineveh by the Assyrian conquerors of Israel. There he goes blind and sends his son Tobias on a long journey to collect a debt from a relative. The angel Raphael is sent by God in the guise of a relative to guide and protect Tobias on the journey.

In the course of the journey, Raphael teaches Tobias how to cure his father's blindness, tells him how to free a virtuous, beautiful, and rich young woman named Sarah from a demon, sees that he marries Sarah, collects the debt, and leads Tobias and Sarah safely home, where Tobit has his sight restored. Finally, he reveals who he is to Tobit and Tobias. If you want your child to be a faithful servant of God and a lover of human beings, concerned for their welfare, you could not choose a better name.

Rebekah

Meaning: from the Hebrew, "flattering"

Variations: Rebecca, Becky, Becca

Most families would be very happy to have a beautiful and thoughtful young daughter, so perhaps with a name like this your child will grow up to be just that. Only one Rebekah is mentioned in the Bible and she was Isaac's cousin. Isaac had been born in Canaan, at Hebron, but when looking for a wife for his son, Abraham wanted to search among his own family. A servant was sent to make enquiries. He met Rebekah and was struck by her beauty and her thoughtfulness. When he discovered that she was the daughter of Abraham's brother, he asked if she would be willing to come back with him to the land of Canaan and marry Isaac. Rebekah readily agreed.

She married Isaac and he loved her dearly. Rebekah had twin sons, Jacob and Esau. Although Esau was the eldest, God made it plain that he intended to bless Jacob and to work through his family. Esau was Isaac's favorite, so when he thought he was dying, Isaac made plans to bless Esau. Rebekah loved Jacob best and helped him to deceive his father so that he received the blessing. But this brought great sorrow to Rebekah, for Esau was so angry that Jacob had to flee, and Rebekah never saw her much-loved son again (see Gen 24–27). Rebekah was a strong-minded person. She readily set out to a foreign country to marry, but these traits led her into deceit later as she tried to get her own way. However, she seems to have been very beautiful and, for the most part, to have had a very happy marriage.

Reuben

Meaning: from the Hebrew, "see, a son"

Reuben was the eldest of the twelve sons of Jacob. Of them all, he seems to have been the most considerate and to have had a rather more sensitive conscience. Becoming jealous of their younger brother Joseph, the ten older brothers seized him, intending to kill him. It was Reuben who persuaded them not to do this, but rather to leave him in a pit (Gen 37:22). Reuben's plan was to return and help Joseph escape later. However, a group of travellers passed by, and the other brothers sold Joseph to them as a slave.

Many years later, when Joseph had become a great leader in Egypt and the brothers travelled there to buy grain, Joseph, whom the brothers did not recognize, insisted that the next time they came they must bring Benjamin (Gen 42:20). Reuben appreciated that if anything happened to Benjamin, his father, who still pined for Joseph, would be left totally desolate. So Reuben offered his own sons as guarantees to his father that he would bring Benjamin safely home. He clearly showed compassion and a more tender heart than the others on a number of occasions.

Rhoda

Meaning: from the Greek, "a rose"

Variations: Rhona, Rosa, Rose, Rosalie, Rosaline, Rosina, Roslyn

This would be a pretty name for a lively girl. Rhoda was a maidservant in Jerusalem, who got the surprise of her life when she went to answer a knock on the door one night. The apostle Peter had been imprisoned by Herod, and a group of very concerned Christians had met to pray for his release in the house where Rhoda worked. As they prayed, Peter was miraculously released and made his way straight to the house. He knocked and Rhoda went to the door, but when Peter called out to her, she was so amazed to hear his voice that she forgot to open it! She rushed back to tell everyone that Peter was there, but they didn't believe her. The knocking continued, and when they did finally open the door and saw Peter for themselves, they were utterly astonished. This lovely, human story is told to us by St. Luke in Acts 12.

Ruby

Meaning: a ruby is a very valuable, clear, deep-red, precious stone. The word comes from the Latin for "red"

If you give your little girl this name, then as she grows up, you might point her to the last chapter of Proverbs in the King James version of the Bible, which describes a virtuous wife by saying "her price is far above rubies"(Proverbs 31). Certainly, the name would express the great value of your daughter.

The prophet Ezekiel, prophesying the downfall of Tyre in a lament, says that Edom traded "fine linen, coral, and rubies" for

Tyrian goods. And in Isaiah, God promises to bring the exiled chosen people back to their homeland and says of the restoration of the people and the land, "I will make your pinnacles of rubies." The value of rubies is used several times in the King James version of the Old Testament as an expression of great worth and preciousness, and wisdom (meaning the knowledge of God) especially is described as being more precious than rubies.

Rufus

Meaning: **from the Latin, "red"**

Variations: Ruskin, Rusty

Wait till you see the color of his hair before using this one! In the New Testament Rufus was one of the Christians in Rome to whom Paul sent greetings in his letter. Rufus' mother had sometimes looked after Paul, and Paul said that she had been like a mother to him. Paul described Rufus as "chosen in the Lord." He must have been a member of a Christian family closely involved with the church (Rom 16:13).

Ruth

Meaning: **a Moabite name probably meaning "friendship"**

Variation: Ruthie

Beauty, loyalty, faithfulness, love, and patience are all characteristics which all parents would love to see in their daughter. The Ruth of the Bible had all these. Ruth was a woman who lived in Moab and married an Israelite man who had moved from Bethlehem because of a famine. Her husband died and her mother-in-law, Naomi, decided to return to Bethlehem. She suggested that Ruth and her other daughter-in-law, whose husband had also died, return to their families and perhaps marry again. However, Ruth professed her devotion to Naomi and insisted that she would go with her and make Naomi's country her country and Naomi's God her God.

Back in Bethlehem, Ruth gleaned in the fields to find food for them both, picking up what had been dropped by the harvesters. The men working in the fields where she gleaned were impressed that she worked so steadily all day and only took short rests. Naomi had a relative called Boaz who was a landowner and a caring and kindly man, and so Ruth went to glean in his fields. Boaz soon befriended Ruth, and the people of Bethlehem told him of all that she had done for Naomi since her husband had died. Soon the two of them were married. Their grandson was David, and so Ruth was among the ancestors of Jesus. Ruth is remembered for her great love for Naomi. She must have been a very pleasant person to know. Her story is found in the Bible in the book of Ruth.

S

Samson

Meaning: from the Hebrew, "sunlight"

Samson is renowned for his immense physical strength, which God had given to him so that he could fight the pagan Philistines. However, Samson was seduced by a beautiful woman named Delilah, to whom the Philistine rulers paid money to betray him. She persuaded him to tell her the secret of his strength, which was his long hair. When he was asleep, one of her servants cut off his hair, and so his strength left him. She handed him over to the Philistines, and they tortured him for a long time and prepared to put him to death. However, while they were making fun of Samson, whom they had now blinded, his strength returned. He leaned on the pillars of the pagan temple in which he was being pilloried and brought the building down, killing himself and the Philistines inside it (see Judges 16).

Samson—a kind of Old Testament "Rambo" character—is perhaps not the ideal role model, but he would give you some exciting bedtime stories to tell your young son!

Samuel

Meaning: from the Hebrew, "asked of God"

Variations: Sam, Sammy

Any mother who has been waiting a long time and praying for a baby ought to think of this name for a baby boy. Samuel's mother had been in just that position, longing for a child, often getting very sad and depressed, but eventually God gave her a child and she called him "asked of God." This child was certainly an answer to prayer.

It is also a wonderful name for any boy if you want him to be reminded of the importance of serving God. Hannah had promised to give her son to the service of God should she ever have one. So from a very early age, Samuel lived in the precincts of the Tent of Meeting (the Tabernacle) under the care of the old priest Eli. One night, Samuel heard God call him. At first he thought it was Eli and ran to him. Eventually the elderly man realized that God was speaking to the child! (See 1 Sam 3) That was the first recorded time when God spoke to Samuel, but God continued to do so, and Samuel became a great prophet.

Samuel spoke God's words to the Israelites and tried to bring them back to God's ways. When they demanded a king, God told Samuel to anoint Saul to be king. Years later, when Saul had forsaken and disobeyed God, Samuel was instructed to seek out and anoint David to be the next king. All through his life Samuel resolutely tried to keep Israel following the ways of God.

Sarah

Meaning: from the Hebrew, "princess"

How many fathers have talked of their little "princess" as they proudly showed off their new young daughter? The biblical Sarah was the wife of Abraham. And what a wonderful wife she was for him! She went with him without question when he knew that God had called him to travel into Canaan; she wandered the land with him; she seems to have agreed to be described as his sister in a situation which led her into great difficulties. She knew that God had promised a son to them but, as they both got older, she was doubtful about the possibility (Gen 17–18).

Nevertheless, she rejoiced greatly when the baby was born and called him Isaac or "laughter." Abraham deeply loved his beautiful wife, and when she died, he mourned and wept for her.

Though he had no other property in the land, he bought a field in which to bury his precious Sarah. Sarah was a great woman who is even recalled in the New Testament as an outstanding example of a fine wife (1 Pet 3:6).

Saul

Meaning: from the Hebrew, "asked"

If you give your child this name you will certainly not be wanting for exciting stories to tell him! Saul, son of Kish, was the first king of Israel, and his story is recounted in 1 Samuel 9–31. Saul was an outstanding young man physically, being a head taller than any other, and he seemed well suited to be the king and leader of the Israelites in battle. But he did not have the faith in God to make him a good king over Israel.

Samuel often brought God's words and instructions to Saul, but time and again Saul ignored them and did as he pleased. Finally, one act of disobedience was so flagrant that Samuel had to tell Saul that as he had rejected God's words, so God had rejected Saul and would choose someone else to be king after him. This resulted in Samuel being sent by God to anoint David. Sadly, Saul spent some unhappy years being jealous of David and trying to kill him. Eventually Saul was critically injured in battle with the Philistines. Afraid that he would be captured, he killed himself. Saul's was a sad story, for he was a man of great potential, and yet he would not commit himself to doing God's work.

We encounter another Saul in the New Testament. He was probably named after King Saul. He was a Pharisee, a very upright man, and deeply antagonistic to the new sect of Christians. However, in an astounding vision on the road to Damascus, he met the risen Lord Jesus and became his devoted follower, spending his whole life serving him (Acts 9). Saul became better known by his Latin name, Paul, which is how we usually know him.

Seth

Meaning: from the Hebrew, possibly "granted" or "appointed"

If you can imagine your baby boy living a long time, then perhaps you should choose this name! Seth, the third son of Adam and Eve, lived for 912 years. He was born after Cain had killed his brother Abel, and Eve named him because she felt God had granted her another son in place of Abel. Seth had a son, and we read that at this time "people began to invoke the name of the LORD" (Gen 4:26). This is probably to show that it was through Seth that the godly line of men and women would continue on earth.

Sharon

Meaning: from the Hebrew, "flat" or "a plain"

Sharon is nowadays frequently used as a girl's name, but in the Bible it is the name of a fertile plain extending from Joppa to Caesarea. It was specially famous for a flower known as the "rose of Sharon." This was possibly a type of crocus and is mentioned in the wonderful biblical love poem known as the Song of Songs (2:1). The flower has also sometimes been used as a symbol of the Lord Jesus, denoting his great beauty.

In the center of the plain was the city of Sharon. In the New Testament the apostle Peter came to this area. In a town called Lydda he healed Aeneas, a man paralyzed for eight years. On seeing this miracle and hearing Peter preach about Jesus, all those living in the area of Sharon came to believe in the good news about Jesus the Savior (Acts 9:35).

This is a lovely name for a daughter, reflecting a beautiful fertile land where a great work of God took place.

Shem

Meaning: from the Hebrew, "name," "renown"

Perhaps no one would actually want to live as long as six hundred years, which is the length of time Shem lived, according to Genesis 11! Most people would want to be known for their good behavior and for doing what was right, and this was certainly true of Shem. He was Noah's first son and so travelled with him on the ark at the time of the terrible flood (Genesis 7). Later his descendants are listed, and it becomes clear that he was a direct ancestor of Abraham and the Israelites, and so part of the godly line of people who continued to worship God.

Shua

Meaning: from the Hebrew, "wealth"

Those who have desired a daughter and are finally blessed with one certainly feel they have been given great wealth, and so this would be an appropriate name for such a longed-for daughter. Two women were called this in the Old Testament. One was married to Judah, but she came from an irreligious family, and tragedy seems to have followed her married life (Gen 38). The other Shua, however, was a member of a leading family in the tribe of Asher. Obviously, she was well known and her brothers were classed as "chief of princes" and "mighty warriors" (1 Chron 7:32, 40).

Silas

Meaning: from the Aramaic for "Saul," "asked"

If you are a world traveller or if you have different cultures in your background, then maybe this would be a good name for your boy. Silas or Silvanus (his Latin name) was a leading member of the early church in Jerusalem. Like the apostle Paul, he was a Jewish Christian with Roman citizenship. Silas travelled with Paul on his second missionary journey and was with him in Philippi when they were both thrown into prison. Their behavior during an earthquake in the night led to the conversion of the jailer. Later, there was confusion among the magistrates when they were informed that both men, as Roman citizens, had been illegally beaten and imprisoned without a fair trial (Acts 15–17).

At times, Silas also acted as secretary to the apostles. For example, Peter's first epistle was written down by Silas (1 Pet 5:12). He was a fine example of a man of good standing and of good education, with a foothold in several cultural worlds—Jewish, Christian, and Roman. All his talents were devoted to the service of Christ. A great person to be called after!

Simeon

Meaning: from the Hebrew, "hearing"

Variations: See Simon

The best-known Simeon in the Bible is introduced in the story of Jesus' early days (Luke 2:25-35). Simeon was already very old, but had been told by God that he would not die until he had seen the Christ. One day he went into the Temple and saw a young couple bringing their baby to present him to God and to make the offerings required for a first son. Simeon, guided by God, recognized that this child was the Christ. He took Jesus in his arms and praised God, saying that now he could die in peace. He foretold that Jesus had come to be a Savior for Gentiles as well as Jews, and spoke specially to Mary about the work of her child and about the sorrow that would come to her. Simeon was a man whose faith in God had gone on undaunted to his old age.

In the Old Testament, another Simeon is mentioned. He was the second son born to Leah and Jacob (Gen 35:23; 1 Chr 2:1). One of the tribes of Israel was therefore named after him. Genesis

29:33 reveals that Leah called him Simeon "because the Lord heard that I am hated." In other words, Simeon was a very special child for Leah, who was feeling unhappy with life and had prayed to God for help.

Simon

Meaning: "Simon" is used as a Greek form of the Hebrew "Simeon," which means "hearing"

Male variation: Sim

Female variation: Simone

Simon was a popular name in the days of the New Testament, and there are nine people mentioned bearing the name. Perhaps, if you used the name for your baby, you would think first of the apostle Peter, whose other name was Simon. One of Jesus' brothers was also named Simon.

Another Simon, a Pharisee, gave a dinner at his home and invited Jesus as a guest. He was horrified when a woman of ill repute approached Jesus and began to bathe his feet (Luke 7:44). Jesus was aware of Simon's thoughts, but he also knew that the woman was expressing her love for him because he had already forgiven her sins. Another Simon, from Cyrene, was in Jerusalem at the time of the Passover and was pulled out of the crowd by the Roman guards to carry Jesus' cross to Golgotha (Mark 15:21).

Simon the tanner lived by the sea in Joppa (Acts 9:43). The apostle Peter was staying in his house when a message came for Peter to go to Caesarea to visit Cornelius. This was the occasion which made the apostles realize that the gospel was for Gentiles as well as Jews.

Solomon

Meaning: from the Hebrew, related to the word for "peace"

Variations: Salman, Salmon

Having a child who will be peaceful and very wise and understanding would be every parent's dream. If you give your son this name, perhaps you might pray that he will have an "understanding mind," like the Solomon of the Bible. The story of his life is told in 1 Kings 1–11. He was the son of King David and seems to have been an attractive personality. When he came to the throne he dedicated himself to God, and so, in a dream, God offered him his choice of gifts. Solomon requested an "understanding mind" (1 Kgs 3:9) which would be able to hear God and respond to the divine will. He also asked for wisdom to be able to discern between good and evil. In other words, he asked for the gifts he felt were necessary to be a good king—he wanted to understand the issues he confronted and to know how to handle them. God's response was one of approval, and God gave him this wisdom, and the wisdom of Solomon soon became proverbial.

Solomon was granted the privilege of building the Temple for God in Jerusalem, and he became an internationally famous leader. His kingdom extended far north and east and south towards Egypt. In many ways his reign, especially the first twenty years, was the "golden age" for Israel. There was peace in the land and the nation's influence spread far and wide. Sadly, later in life Solomon seems to have become rather proud and to have left God out of the picture. His "understanding mind" had left him, and the last few years of his reign depict his declining glory.

Sophia

Meaning: from the Greek, "wisdom"

Variations: Sophie, Sofie, Sonya

Giving your daughter this name will probably not guarantee that she will grow up to be "wise," but who knows? It won't hurt to try! The word *sophia* appears in the New Testament and in the Greek version of the Old Testament, but not as a person's name. It simply means "wisdom." The Bible often contrasts what it calls the "wisdom of the world" with the "wisdom of God" (see 1 Cor 1:21 and 2 Cor 1:12). This contrast simply refers to whether people follow what God has commanded or follow their instincts or the way that the world around them seems to be going, which is often set against God's order for things. Perhaps giving a child this name will let you teach her what the difference is between God's ways and other ways.

Stachys

Meaning: from the Greek, "an ear of grain"

This is sometimes used as a girl's name today, but in the Bible it is a man's name. Stachys was a dear friend of the apostle Paul. He lived in Rome and was greeted by Paul in Romans 16:9.

Stephen

Meaning: from the Hebrew, "wealth" or "crown"

Male variations: Steve, Steven, Stevie, Steven, Esteban

Female variations: Stephanie, Steffie, Stephana

Children can be the crowning joy of a family, and so a name that reflects this idea may be just what you are looking for. This name is deservedly very popular. The Stephen mentioned in the New Testament has been loved and remembered down through the ages by all Christians, for he was the first person to be killed for his faith in Jesus Christ. He was one of a group of seven men chosen to be deacons and to help the apostles in administrative work in the early days of the church in Jerusalem.

As well as doing such work, Stephen was deeply involved in the preaching of the gospel and the growth of the church. He also did miraculous wonders which gave his preaching great credibility. His activities aroused fierce opposition from some Jews, and they contrived his arrest, charging him with teaching things contrary to Moses' teaching. They brought him before the Council, and Stephen made a great speech defending his faith. But when he accused them of failing to recognize Christ and said that he could see Jesus standing at God's right hand in heaven, they dragged him outside and stoned him to death. As he died, Stephen prayed that God would forgive them. The story of Stephen's faith and courage and of his brave death needs to be told to any child given this name. This part of Acts (chapter 7 especially) always provides good bedtime stories!

Susanna

Meaning: **from the Hebrew, "lily"**

Variations: Sue, Susan, Susanne, Suzanne, Suzette, Suzy, Shushana

This would be a lovely name for a little girl, perhaps reminding you of the flowers of spring and the joy of life. In Luke 8:3 we find that Susanna was one of a group of women who loved and followed Jesus. As Jesus travelled round, these women supported him and his disciples financially from their own means. Perhaps Susanna was a merchant; in any case, she used her wealth for the work of God's kingdom.

Another Susanna is very well known; she appears in the Greek version of the book of Daniel. Susanna lived in Babylon with her husband Joakim. She was "a very beautiful woman and one who feared the Lord." Two elders of the people, who had been appointed judges, looked on Susanna's beauty and were overcome with passion. They turned from God and decided to entrap Susanna so she would have to do their will. When they did this, she told them she would rather die than sin against God.

The two wicked elders told the people that they had witnessed Susanna being unfaithful to her husband. The people believed the elders since they had no way of knowing how evil the two men were, and condemned Susanna to death. Susanna wept and cried out to God. As she was being led to her execution, Daniel shouted for them to stop. Then he exposed the lies of the two elders, who were executed for falsely accusing Susanna, and all praised God who had spared the shedding of innocent blood.

Susanna was a woman who loved God so much she was willing to die rather than betray that love. She is certainly someone your daughter could look up to.

T

Tabitha

Meaning: from the Aramaic, "gazelle"

Tabitha, who was also called Dorcas, was a Christian living in Joppa. She was very involved in the work amongst the poor and made many garments for them. She became ill and died, and the other disciples sent for the apostle Peter. He came and prayed over her, and she was restored to life. Because of this miracle, many people believed. Tabitha was a busy and loving woman and was in turn loved herself: a happy example for your daughter (Acts 9:36-39).

Tamar

Meaning: from the Hebrew, "date tree"

Because a date tree stood tall and proud and its fruit was so highly valued, this name came to imply everything that was good and perfect, so this may be just the right name for a new daughter. Perhaps you will think it better to remember the real meaning of the name rather than hope she grows up like the Tamars we find in the Bible! One, who was the daughter-in-law of Judah, had a very sad life. Two of her sons died and she was not well treated by the rest of the family (Gen 38). Another Tamar also had an unhappy background. She was one of King David's daughters and very beautiful, but she was later raped by her own half-brother (2 Sam 13). However, another Tamar was the daughter of Absalom, and we are told that she became a beautiful women. Perhaps this is the one you would do well to remember if you use this name (2 Sam 14:27).

Thomas

Meaning: from the Aramaic, "twin"

Male variations: Tom, Tommie, Tommy, Tomás, Tam

Female variations: Thomasina, Tommie, Tammy, Tamara, Tamsin

Thomas has always been a popular name. Many people can easily identify with this character who initially doubted and then later changed his position. He was one of Jesus' disciples. He is sometimes called "doubting Thomas." Because he was not present when Jesus appeared to the disciples after his resurrection, Thomas was very sceptical about it. However, later he both saw and touched Jesus and was immediately convinced that he was truly God. Indeed, in the end Thomas made one of the strongest statements in the New Testament about Jesus being God. Seeing Jesus, he worshiped him and said to him, "My Lord and my God." (John 20:28).

Timothy

Meaning: from the Greek, "honoring God" or "precious to God"

Male variations: Tim, Timmy, Timmie

Female variations: Timothea, Timmie

What a fine character for any child to look up to as he grows up! Even as a young man, Timothy was very highly regarded and took on great responsibilities in the early church. He was the son of a Jewish mother and a Greek father. His mother and grandmother became Christians when the apostle Paul preached in Lystra, and they brought Timothy up to know the Bible and to serve God. When Paul came back to Lystra, he took Timothy along on his missionary travels and then frequently mentioned him in his letters.

Timothy was sent on visits to many churches and often took messages from the apostle. For a time he was left in charge of the church at Ephesus. Paul wrote two letters to Timothy encouraging him and offering help and advice in pastoring churches. Timothy was perhaps a rather timid person, lacking in self-confidence, and he even seems to have had some stomach problems (1 Tim 5:23), but he was obviously very likeable and popular with the members of the various churches and very highly regarded by Paul (Phil 2:22). He would be a fine example to your small son or daughter. The name has always been a very popular one. (See the letters to Timothy in the New Testament).

Titus

Meaning: **not known. A Latin name perhaps derived from a Greek root**

Not a common boy's name these days, but it sounds good, and certainly, the Titus of the Bible would be a good role model! He was one of Paul's companions in his missionary work. Paul put great trust in him and left him in Crete to organize and establish the leadership of the church there. Paul wrote a letter of instructions for the work (see the letter to Titus in the New Testament). Titus was also in Corinth for a while, assisting the church in a variety of ways, including the raising of money to send to the church in Jerusalem, which was in need. Paul records how great a comfort it was to see Titus again when he returned from Corinth. Titus was an excellent leader. He was faithful and trustworthy and could both lead and teach others.

Tobiah

Meaning: **from the Hebrew, "God is good"**

Variations: Tobias, Tobit, Toby

Provided you can get away from thinking of a "Toby jug," then this could be a really lovely name for any boy. The name is full of special meaning and captures something of the excitement people feel when God has given them something they have wanted. No doubt parents who used this name in biblical times did so because they felt their child was a demonstration to them of God's goodness, so if you feel like that about your baby, then this will be a name well worth considering.

There are two Tobiahs mentioned in the books of Ezra and Nehemiah. One was a faithful Israelite who was thrilled to have returned from the exile in Babylon and to be back in Israel, where he could once again worship God in the Temple and take part in rebuilding it and the walls of Jerusalem (Ezra 2:60; Neh 7:62). The other Tobiah lived in the same period of history but seemed to prefer to support the Persian overlords rather than to work with Nehemiah and the others in trying to restore Jerusalem to its former glory. He did not worship God with them either (Neh 2; 4:3-15).

There are two other Tobiahs in the Greek version of the Old Testament, called the Septuagint. There they are called Tobit and Tobias. Tobit was an Israelite who, with his wife Anna and son Tobias lived in exile in Nineveh after the fall of Israel to the Assyrians. He was devoted to God and cared for the poor. He also buried his fellow Israelites despite the prohibition of the king of Assyria, and because of this, he lost his wealth. To add to his sorrow, he also lost his sight.

Tobit sent his son, Tobias, to collect a debt owed by a relative in Media, and the angel Raphael, who assumed the appearance of another relative, Azariah, guided Tobias on the journey. Instructed by the angel, Tobias freed Sarah, the beautiful and pious daughter of Raguel, from a terrible demon through prayer. Raguel, who was very rich and admired Tobias, gave him Sarah in marriage and made him his heir. Together, Tobias and Sarah returned to Nineveh, guided by Raphael, who had collected the debt. Again under the angel's instruction, Tobias cured his father's blindness.

Both Tobit and Tobias were men who loved God and faithfully prayed to God, in good times and bad. They performed acts of kindness because of their devotion to God. These are two fine examples for any son. You can read the whole story in the book of Tobit.

Tryphena

Meaning: from the Greek, "delicate" or "dainty"

This woman is greeted by the apostle Paul at the end of his Letter to the Romans. She is mentioned along with another woman called Tryphosa. They were probably among the quite large group of women mentioned in the epistles, who were wealthy and either merchants or women of leisure (Rom 16:12). Many such women had become Christians and had given their time and money to help the growing young churches. Such women are well worth remembering, and although either of these names would be most unusual, they do have a very pretty sound.

Tryphosa

Meaning: from the Greek, perhaps "delicate"

See "Tryphena." This would be an interesting girl's name, although she might have trouble spelling it!

Z

Zaccheus

Meaning: from the Hebrew, "pure"

Variations: Zack, Zak

Zaccheus lived in the city of Jericho, where he was a tax-collector, so he was despised by his fellow Jews, who simply saw him as a pawn in the hands of the Romans. One day he heard that Jesus was going to be walking his way. He was very short and the crowds were large, so he climbed into a sycamore tree so that he could see over the throngs of people. When Jesus passed, he looked up and asked Zaccheus to come down and take him back to his house to eat. The crowd were amazed that Jesus should take time out with such a man, and especially that he should eat with him, which was a sign of social acceptance. But no one was more amazed than Zaccheus himself! He did as he was asked, and was so moved by Jesus doing this that he repented of his sin. He then showed his complete change of heart by paying back any money that he had wrongly taken and giving half of his possessions to the poor. This story is a lovely reminder to people that Jesus came to bring love and forgiveness to everyone, no matter what their background and no matter how much they may be despised by others (Luke 19:1-10).

Zadok

Meaning: from the Hebrew, "righteous"

This name is probably never used for a boy these days, but it is worth including here. Maybe you could start a trend! In the Bible, nine men had this name, and they were all great servants of God.

The most famous was a priest who lived during the reign of King David. He helped David with the temple worship and stood by him even through the most difficult times in David's reign (for the whole story see 2 Sam 8–19). He was loyal to David and faithful to God. God therefore rewarded him by allowing his descendants to be the only God-appointed legitimate heirs to the priesthood (Ezek 40:46).

Zebedee

Meaning: from the Hebrew, "gift of God"

Variation: Zeb

This name would have a clear and special meaning for parents who think of their son as a "gift from God." Just one person has this name in the New Testament, and he was the father of two of Jesus' twelve apostles, James and John. He was a fisherman in Galilee and owned his own boat on the lake (Matt 4:21-22). His family may well have supported Jesus financially during his ministry.

Zechariah

Meaning: from the Hebrew, "God has remembered"

Variations: Zachariah, Zachary, Zacharias, Zeke, Zach, Zak

If you want the most popular name in the Bible, then this is it! There are twenty-eight different characters with this name. It is not surprising that this became a popular name, for its meaning is full of significance for people who love God. It was one of the great beliefs of the Israelite people that their God always "remembered them" and that their God is a "covenant God" who has made promises to the people—promises about their nation and land, and about their forgiveness and God's presence with them. It was therefore part of their faith that God was a God who "remembered" the divine promises. When God asks Moses to lead the Israelites out of Egypt to the promised land, God says, in effect, "I have remembered my people and my promises to Abraham" (Exod 6:5). When Mary sings praise to God because Jesus is soon to be born as the long-awaited king whom God had promised, she says,

> "He has helped his servant Israel,
>   in remembrance of his mercy" (Luke 1:54).

But even more interesting is the song that the father of John the Baptist sang when he heard the same news—and his name was Zechariah!

> "He has raised up a mighty savior for us
>   . . . .
> he has shown the mercy promised to our ancestors,
>   and has remembered his holy covenant,
> the oath that he swore to our ancestor Abraham" (Luke 1:69-73).

No wonder, then, that people loved this name. Many who bore the name were priests and Levites, but the most famous is a prophet who wrote one of the books of the Old Testament. He prophesied around 520 B.C.E., after the Israelites had been in exile in Babylon. He looked forward to a great time when God would fulfill still more of the divine promises, and when God would be seen to be ruler over all the nations. (See the book of Zechariah.)